Fiscal Affairs Department

From Stimulus to Consolidation: Revenue and Expenditure Policies in Advanced and Emerging Economies

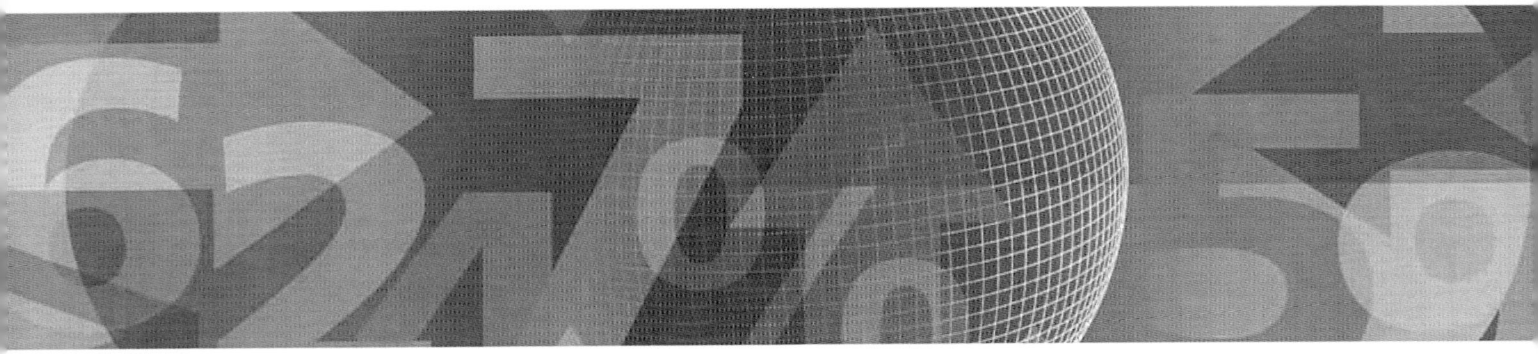

A Staff Team Led by Benedict Clements, Victoria Perry, and Juan Toro

I N T E R N A T I O N A L   M O N E T A R Y   F U N D

Production: IMF Multimedia Services Division
Typesetting: Alicia Etchebarne-Bourdin

Cataloging-in-Publication Data

From stimulus to consolidation : revenue and expenditure policies in advanced and emerging economies/a staff team led by Benedict Clements, Victoria Perry, and Juan Toro—Washington, D.C.: International Monetary Fund, 2010.

p. ; cm.

Includes bibliographical references.
ISBN 978-1-61635-042-0

1. Expenditures, Public. 2. Government spending policy. 3. Revenue. 4. Taxation. I. Clements, Benedict J. II. Perry, Victoria J. III. Toro, Juan. IV. International Monetary Fund.
HJ7461.F76 2010

Please send orders to:
International Monetary Fund, Publication Services
P.O. Box 92780, Washington, D.C. 20090, U.S.A.
Telephone: (202) 623-7430 Fax: (202) 623-7201
E-mail: publications@imf.org
Internet: www.imfbookstore.org

Contents

Preface

An extraordinary global effort on fiscal and monetary policy has been required to support economic activity in the wake of the Great Recession. A key challenge now facing the world economy is to ensure that economic growth resumes in a strong, sustained, and balanced way. As the recovery becomes entrenched, policymakers will need to start reducing public debt ratios to more prudent levels.

This paper by the Fiscal Affairs Department (FAD) aims to assist International Monetary Fund (IMF) member countries in this endeavor by providing a strategy for fiscal adjustment that can help support sustainable growth over the longer term. It was presented at an IMF Executive Board seminar in May 2010. It discusses a menu of specific revenue and spending policy measures that could be considered to implement this strategy. On the spending side, the paper suggests a two-pronged strategy focused on stabilizing pension and public health spending ratios to GDP and reducing other outlays, including public wages, untargeted social spending, and subsidies. On the revenue side, particular attention is given to measures that could raise revenues by reducing existing distortions in the tax system.

Many people have contributed to this paper. The work was overseen by Gerd Schwartz and coordinated by Benedict Clements, Victoria Perry, and Juan Toro. The main contributors to the paper were Ernesto Crivelli, Philip Daniel, Luc Eyraud, Borja Gracia, Jack Grigg, Graham Harrison, Benjamin Jones, Izabela Karpowicz, Adam Leive, Oana Luca, Mario Mansour, Thornton Matheson, Priscilla Muthoora, John Norregaard, Geremia Palomba, Joana Pereira, Patrick Petit, John Piotrowski, Mauricio Soto, Anita Tuladhar, Ricardo Varsano, and Asegedech WoldeMariam. Beulah David, Latoya McDonald, Jeff Pichocki, and Mileva Radisavljević helped with administrative and editorial work. Joanne Blake and her team in the External

Relations Department helped turn the original paper into this Departmental Paper. Helpful inputs and comments were provided by many colleagues in FAD.

Overview

This paper identifies policy tools to support fiscal consolidation in the years ahead. Its starting point is the analysis in recent papers by IMF staff describing strategies for fiscal consolidation (Ali Abbas and others, 2010; and IMF, 2010a), which showed that on current trends, general government debt in advanced countries would rise 36 percentage points of GDP during 2007–14, and that age-related spending (health and pension) would rise rapidly later, further adding to fiscal pressures. Trends are more favorable in emerging economies, but adjustments are needed there too.

The consolidation strategy, particularly in advanced countries, should aim to stabilize age-related spending in relation to GDP, reduce non-age-related expenditure ratios, and increase revenues in an efficient manner. The precise mix will vary across countries, but given the high level of taxation in advanced countries and recent increases in spending, a relatively stronger effort is needed on expenditures.

On the spending side, bold reforms are needed to offset the projected rise in age-related outlays, particularly health care. In pensions, a further increase in statutory retirement ages of two years could offset the projected rise of spending of 1 percentage point of GDP over the next 20 years in advanced economies. In health, the challenge is greater, and has so far been underestimated, particularly in Europe. New staff projections show that health spending could rise by 3½ percentage points of GDP over the next 20 years in advanced countries. Reforms are needed to address supply-side incentives, limit public benefits, or reduce the demand for public health services. But while many countries have managed to reform significantly their pension systems, the difficulty of health reform is underscored by the dearth of prominent reforms in advanced countries aimed primarily at reducing spending.

In other spending areas, in addition to allowing stimulus spending increases to expire, a possible policy goal could be to freeze spending in real per capita terms for 10 years. This would save 3–3½ percentage points of GDP. It would require deep spending reforms. Containing the wage bill has in the past proved to be key to successful fiscal consolidation. Expenditure on social benefits could be reduced, without sacrificing equity objectives, through better targeting. Subsidy spending should also be lowered, including for petroleum products, which absorb about 1 percent of world GDP. There may also be scope for savings on military spending.

On the revenue side, boosting revenues in a global economy requires strengthening broad-based taxes on relatively immobile bases and improving tax compliance, including through better international cooperation. Relatively efficient measures could yield perhaps 2.8 percent of GDP (on a weighted average basis) in G-7 countries from: increasing the yield of the VAT by eliminating exemptions and reduced rates; further developing property taxes; increasing excise rates within the scope of rates already applicable in comparable countries; and introducing (and capturing revenues from) efficient carbon pricing in the United States and Europe. A menu of additional measures—for instance, introducing VAT in the United States, and doubling the very low VAT rate in Japan—could further raise revenues by 4.5 and 2.6 percent of GDP, respectively, in those countries. There is also scope for stronger income taxation, in part to address equity objectives, though efficiency concerns loom larger there.

The potential for improving tax compliance is also significant. Tax systems in many countries suffer from pervasive tax abuse through informality, aggressive tax planning, offshore tax abuse, fraud, and increasing tax debt as a result of the crisis and recession. Improving tax compliance will require enhancing international collaboration in tax information exchange and transparency, strengthening risk management approaches, intensifying use of modern information technology to manage tax compliance, tackling endemic abuses to improve the taxpaying culture in some countries, and improving legal frameworks. Extra revenue equivalent to 0.7 percent of GDP could be collected by reducing the VAT gap in G-20 countries in the coming years.

CHAPTER

1 Introduction

This paper seeks to identify policy tools that could be used for fiscal consolidation in advanced and emerging countries in the wake of the global financial crisis. Issues related to the size and timing of fiscal adjustment, policy coordination, and demand management were addressed in previous papers (Ali Abbas and others, 2010; and IMF, 2010a).

The magnitude of the challenge to revenue and expenditure policies is large, including in light of projected increases in age-related spending. The effects of the crisis have been severe, particularly in advanced countries:

- In advanced countries, primary deficits rose by 7½ percentage points of GDP between 2007 and 2010, reflecting underlying spending increases, stimulus measures, and cyclical factors (Ali Abbas and others, 2010; and IMF, 2010a, 2010b).[1] These increases have come on top of an already rising spending trend, in real per capita terms and also relative to GDP, during this decade (Table 1.1a). Revenues have declined in real terms owing to the collapse in assets prices, financial sector profits, reduced output, and possibly, reduced tax compliance. As a result, general government gross debt is projected to rise by 36 percentage points of GDP between 2007 and 2014. To reduce it to, say, 60 percent of GDP by 2030, an average improvement in the structural primary balance of 8¾ percentage points of GDP on a PPP-weighted basis (unweighted average,

[1]All country group averages are purchasing power parity (PPP) GDP weighted throughout the text, unless otherwise noted.

4¾ percentage points of GDP) would be required between 2010 and 2020 (Ali Abbas and others, 2010; and IMF, 2010b).[2] This would have to be achieved at a time when age-related spending (health and pensions) will tend to rise by about 4–5 percentage points of GDP.

- In the emerging economies, revenue growth in 2008–10 has experienced a marked slowdown from the rapid increases observed in the pre-crisis period (2001–07). Primary spending has also been rising rapidly in real terms at a slightly faster pace compared to the pre-crisis period (Table 1.1b). In these countries, the need for adjustment is less severe—on average, 2¾ percentage points of GDP, if the goal is to reduce public debt to a ratio of 40 percent of GDP by 2030.

The adjustments needed to achieve these debt targets vary substantially across countries. For example, among advanced economies, about two-thirds face primary adjustment needs lower than 5 percentage points of GDP, while one-fifth require adjustments greater than 8 percentage points of GDP.

---

[2]For advanced countries, adjustment numbers under this illustrative scenario are calculated based on a target gross general government debt-to-GDP ratio of 60 percent, equal to the G-20 advanced countries' median prior to the crisis. For countries whose debt ratios are projected to be below this threshold in 2012, the required adjustment is calculated as the change in the cyclically adjusted primary balance (CAPB) necessary to stabilize the debt at its post-crisis (2012) level. For these countries, adjustment at least sufficient to eliminate any CAPB deficit in 2010 will be required, to ensure that the debt ratio does not increase indefinitely. Many countries also report government debt ratios net of financial assets. Gross and net debt are both important indicators of fiscal trends. Gross debt ratios are often regarded as a better indicator for assessing rollover risks. For assessing solvency risks, or for evaluating the impact of debt accumulation on, say, interest rates or overall economic performance, the superiority of gross over net debt is less clear cut. One key advantage of focusing on gross debt in cross-country comparisons is that the definition of this variable is fairly consistent across countries. The definition of net debt is less uniform, due to different treatment of assets. Be this as it may, results of calculations based on targeting a net debt ratio of 45 percent of GDP (the advanced G-20 median for net debt prior to the crisis) are similar to those presented here: differences in the cumulative adjustment required over the next 10 years exceed 1 percent of GDP only for Canada (1.7 percent), Iceland (1.3 percent), and Ireland (1.2 percent), where for all three the adjustment to achieve the net debt target is smaller than that needed to reach the gross debt target. Additional information on these calculations, including a full scenario targeting net debt, is presented in the May issue of the *Fiscal Monitor* (IMF, 2010b).

Table 1.1a. Advanced Economies: Revenue, Expenditure, and Illustrative Adjustment

(General government, unless otherwise noted)

	Illustrative Adjustment	Revenue, 2007	Primary Exp., 2007	Revenue 2001-07	Revenue 2008-10	Primary Expenditure 2001-07	Primary Expenditure 2008-10	GDP 2001-07	GDP 2008-10	Population 2001-2007
	(In percent of GDP)					*(In average annual real growth)*				
Australia	5.2	35.5	33.5	3.1	-1.6	3.6	4.3	3.4	2.2	1.4
Austria	4.7	48.1	45.9	1.5	-0.8	1.3	2.1	2.1	-0.1	0.5
Belgium	4.7	48.2	44.5	1.7	0.0	2.6	3.5	1.9	-0.4	0.5
Canada	4.4	40.7	34.9	1.6	-2.2	3.2	4.2	2.6	0.3	1.0
Cyprus	5.6	45.5	39.1	7.7	-3.2	5.9	5.0	3.6	0.4	1.7
Czech Republic	3.7	41.9	41.4	5.9	-1.3	4.7	1.7	4.5	-0.1	0.1
Denmark	4.3	55.7	49.4	1.6	-5.6	1.4	0.8	1.6	-1.6	0.3
Finland	4.4	47.4	40.8	2.3	-2.0	3.1	5.1	3.2	-1.9	0.3
France	8.3	49.6	49.6	1.7	-1.5	2.1	2.2	1.8	-0.1	0.7
Germany	4.0	43.9	40.9	0.4	-1.9	0.9	2.8	1.2	-0.9	0.0
Greece	9.2	40.4	40.0	3.3	-1.3	4.4	4.6	4.2	-1.3	0.2
Hong Kong	3.8	22.2	14.5	8.9	-8.8	1.9	8.1	4.9	1.4	0.5
Iceland	0.9	47.7	39.7	5.3	-9.0	4.3	-3.1	4.6	-2.9	1.4
Ireland	9.8	35.8	34.9	5.7	-5.1	8.6	3.7	5.5	-3.9	2.0
Israel	2.8	44.6	40.2	2.6	-3.0	2.2	1.1	3.0	2.6	1.9
Italy	4.1	46.4	42.9	1.5	-2.2	2.2	0.9	1.1	-1.9	0.5
Japan	13.1	31.0	30.9	2.2	-2.8	0.2	4.2	1.6	-1.5	0.1
Korea [1]	-3.3	25.0	19.4	6.2	0.4	6.7	5.1	4.7	2.3	0.4
Luxembourg	6.4	39.9	36.0	3.0	-1.3	3.8	5.0	4.3	-0.7	1.3
Malta	2.2	40.3	39.1	3.9	1.6	2.5	3.7	1.8	0.2	0.8
Netherlands	5.5	45.5	43.0	1.7	-1.0	2.8	3.5	1.9	-0.3	0.6
New Zealand [1]	0.9	33.7	29.9	3.3	-3.5	3.3	3.5	3.3	0.4	1.3
Norway	0.1	58.7	39.7	3.4	-1.5	3.0	3.4	2.3	0.4	0.7
Portugal	7.8	43.2	42.9	2.1	-3.0	2.1	1.4	1.1	-0.8	0.6
Singapore	4.7	25.4	12.2	3.2	-5.9	-1.6	22.8	5.6	1.6	1.9
Slovak Republic	4.1	28.8	29.0	6.5	5.4	3.6	9.2	6.2	1.8	0.0
Slovenia	4.0	40.5	39.2	4.4	-0.1	4.0	4.7	4.4	-1.0	0.1
Spain	9.4	41.1	37.6	4.5	-5.7	4.1	4.0	3.4	-1.1	1.4
Sweden	2.3	53.6	48.0	2.0	-2.4	2.3	2.5	2.8	-1.1	0.4
Switzerland	-0.8	36.6	33.2	2.2	-0.3	2.6	2.9	2.0	0.6	0.2
United Kingdom	9.0	37.8	38.3	2.5	-2.6	4.3	4.1	2.6	-1.1	0.5
United States [2]	12.0	33.9	33.6	2.4	-3.2	3.8	5.3	2.6	0.3	1.0
Average	8.7	37.4	35.8	2.5	-2.6	3.0	4.3	2.4	-0.2	0.7
Advanced G-20	9.3	36.4	35.3	2.2	-2.6	3.0	4.3	2.3	-0.2	0.7

Sources: World Economic Outlook (WEO) database; and IMF staff estimates.

Note: For a description of illustrative adjustment, see footnote 2 of text and notes for Figure 1.1. The illustrative adjustment refers to the change in the cyclically adjusted primary balance needed to stabilize debt at the end-2012 level by 2030 if the respective debt-to-GDP ratio is less than 60 percent (no shading) or to bring the debt ratio to 60 percent in 2030 (shaded). Figures for Greece incorporate latest IMF program data that assume an adjustment of 7.6 percent of GDP in 2010. For Australia, the figures do not take account of the latest federal government budget, released on May 11, which envisages a return to federal government surpluses by 2012–13.

[1]Central government.

[2]Earliest year consistent WEO revenue and expenditure growth series available: 2002.

Table 1.1b. Emerging Economies: Revenue, Expenditure, and Illustrative Adjustment

(General government, unless otherwise noted)

	Illustrative Adjustment	Revenue, 2007	Primary Exp., 2007	Revenue 2001-07	Revenue 2008-10	Primary Expenditure 2001-07	Primary Expenditure 2008-10	GDP 2001-07	GDP 2008-10	Population 2001-2007
	(In percent of GDP)			*(In average annual real growth)*						
Argentina [1]	1.6	31.5	28.8	7.5	6.2	6.5	10.0	3.8	3.7	1.0
Brazil [1,2]	-2.1	35.7	32.3	4.4	4.3	4.4	4.5	3.8	3.4	1.3
Bulgaria	-0.8	40.7	36.1	6.4	-2.8	6.0	2.1	5.6	0.3	-1.3
Chile	3.0	29.4	19.9	7.6	-4.3	2.0	11.1	4.3	2.3	1.2
China [3]	3.1	20.5	19.1	16.8	9.2	12.9	16.2	10.4	9.4	0.6
Colombia [1]	1.1	27.1	24.1	6.1	-1.5	4.8	2.5	4.9	1.6	1.2
Croatia	0.1	40.7	40.2	5.0	-3.2	3.4	-2.1	4.7	-1.2	0.2
Egypt	8.5	27.7	30.0	4.1	0.9	7.3	2.1	4.6	5.6	2.2
Hungary	-1.3	44.9	45.8	3.6	-2.1	4.8	-3.1	3.7	-2.0	-0.2
India	7.0	22.8	21.7	11.5	3.1	7.4	10.8	7.3	7.3	1.6
Indonesia [3]	0.3	18.5	17.7	8.7	0.1	9.8	2.3	5.1	5.5	1.4
Malaysia	6.8	25.5	26.5	7.8	2.6	7.1	6.1	5.1	2.5	2.1
Mexico [1]	0.5	21.4	20.1	4.0	0.0	4.1	3.3	2.5	-0.4	1.1
Nigeria	6.0	28.4	28.4	3.7	4.2	8.8	11.3	9.7	6.2	2.8
Pakistan	1.3	15.3	16.5	6.3	1.5	10.2	-0.5	5.2	2.3	2.0
Peru	1.1	20.9	16.0	7.6	2.7	3.2	13.0	5.4	5.6	1.6
Philippines [3]	0.8	15.8	13.1	5.3	0.8	2.9	5.6	5.0	2.8	2.1
Poland	7.2	40.3	39.9	4.9	2.3	4.7	6.7	4.1	3.1	-0.1
Romania [4]	2.1	32.3	34.6	8.8	0.4	8.9	2.6	6.1	0.1	-0.3
Russia	1.6	40.0	32.7	8.2	-3.5	8.7	5.2	6.6	0.4	-0.3
Saudi Arabia [3]	1.7	50.1	32.9	6.2	0.6	4.3	10.9	3.4	2.7	2.5
South Africa	3.4	28.4	24.6	6.7	0.0	6.8	9.0	4.3	1.5	1.0
Turkey [5]	0.4	31.7	27.4	9.0	1.5	8.8	5.4	6.9	0.3	1.2
Ukraine	2.2	41.8	43.1	11.2	-3.9	11.6	-3.7	7.7	-3.5	-0.7
Average	2.7	26.9	24.5	10.4	3.7	8.7	9.3	7.0	5.1	0.9
Emerging G-20	2.6	26.3	23.5	11.3	4.4	9.2	10.4	7.3	5.6	0.9

Sources: WEO; and IMF staff estimates.

Note: For a description of illustrative adjustment, see footnote 2 of text and notes for Figure 1.1. The illustrative adjustment refers to the change in the cyclically adjusted primary balance needed to stabilize debt at the end-2012 level by 2030 if the respective debt-to-GDP ratio is less than 40 percent or to bring the debt ratio to 40 percent in 2030.

[1]Nonfinancial public sector.

[2]Earliest year consistent WEO revenue and expenditure growth series available: 2002.

[3]Central government.

[4]Earliest year consistent WEO revenue and expenditure growth series available: 2005.

[5]Earliest year consistent WEO revenue and expenditure growth series available: 2003.

These differences reflect variations, not only in initial debt positions, but also initial primary structural balances. The adjustments needed to offset age-related spending pressures also vary, depending not only on demographics and income levels, but also the coverage and generosity of the systems (Figure 1.1).

The paper is structured as follows. The rest of this introduction sets out general considerations for balancing revenue and spending measures to achieve fiscal consolidation. Chapter 2 identifies reform options for public spending, also based on new staff projections for age-related spending for a large number of advanced and emerging economies. Chapter 3 considers reform options in tax policy and administration.

Balancing Revenue and Expenditure Measures in Adjustment Strategies

The appropriate mix of adjustment measures will depend on various factors, although, on average, higher reliance on spending cuts will likely be needed, particularly in advanced countries. The literature generally finds expenditure-based adjustments to have been more successful.[3] Looking ahead, the mix between revenue and expenditure measures should reflect:

- *Current spending and revenue levels.* With tax burdens high in many advanced countries, there may be limited scope to raise tax rates without adverse effects on economic efficiency, with some exceptions, notably carbon pricing. This—together with the fact that the stimulus measures consisted primarily of spending increases, as well as the need to offset the trend increase in age-related spending—will imply higher reliance on spending cuts. But the extent of this will vary with preexisting tax design and implementation: closing the gaps in a porous VAT, for instance, can provide a relatively efficient source of substantial revenue, even in countries with relatively high tax-to-GDP ratios.

[3]See Ali Abbas and others (2010) for a review of the literature.

Figure 1.1. Illustrative Fiscal Adjustment and Projected Age-Related Spending Increases in 2011–30

(In percent of GDP)

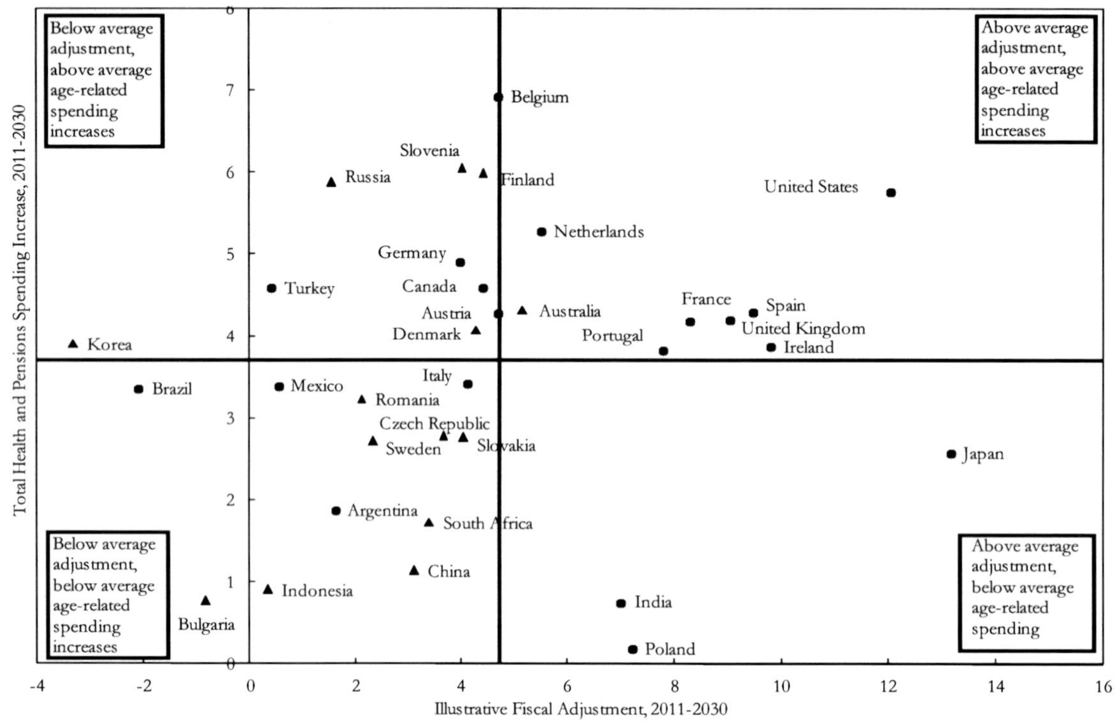

Source: IMF staff estimates.

Notes: Fiscal adjustment refers to improvements in the cyclically adjusted primary balance needed to achieve the illustrative gross general government debt target. Circles indicate debt ratios above 60 percent for advanced economies and 40 percent for emerging economies, projected at end 2012; triangles indicate debt ratios below 60 percent for advanced economies and 40 percent for emerging economies, projected for the same period. For Japan, the target is 200 percent of gross debt (close to the pre-crisis level); even with this less ambitious target, Japan has the highest needed adjustment among all countries. For Greece (not shown), the comparable figures for required adjustment and health and pension spending increases are 9.2 and 7.6 percent of GDP, respectively; this assumes an adjustment of 7.6 percent of GDP is implemented in 2010. For Australia, the figures do not take account of the latest federal government budget, released on May 11, which envisages a return to federal government surpluses by 2012–13. The analysis is illustrative and makes some simplifying assumptions: in particular, up to 2015, an interest rate-growth rate differential of 0 percent is assumed, broadly in line with WEO assumptions, after 2015 differential is 1 percent for all countries. For details on methodology and the country-specific estimates, see Ali Abbas and others (2010), IMF (2010b), and footnote 2 in the text. For a description of projected increases in age-related spending, see Chapter 2. The vertical and horizontal lines represent unweighted averages.

- *Size of the needed adjustment.* Where this is large, substantial measures are likely needed on both the revenue and expenditure sides. The unprecedented magnitude of the required adjustment will most likely also require revenue measures in many countries. In most advanced economies, for example, a freeze on real per capita expenditures (other than health and pension outlays) over the next 10 years would be insufficient to generate the needed adjustment as shown in the illustrative scenario (Ali Abbas and others, 2010).
- *Impact of reform measures on growth and equity.* This would suggest a strong emphasis on reform of inefficient, poorly targeted, and inequitable public spending. In some cases, offsetting measures, such as stronger and better-targeted social safety nets, may be needed to address the effects of reforms.
- *Socio-political views on the role of government.* Where there is consensus on a relatively larger role for government, basing fiscal consolidation on revenue expansion may find broader support.

Reflecting these considerations, the focus of country adjustment strategies will vary (Table 1.2). The guidelines below should be seen in the context of strategies for fiscal consolidation, rather than longer-term development goals that could influence revenue and expenditure plans:

- Where both adjustment needs and tax effort are relatively low, revenue-raising is naturally the main focus (Indonesia and Mexico).
- Where adjustment needs are low and the impulse from spending has been high, or the tax level is relatively high, adjustment should rely more on expenditure reductions (Argentina, Brazil, Russia, Saudi Arabia, Sweden, and Turkey)—including through improvements in the efficiency of spending. In addition, where there is scope for improving revenues, reforms should include measures in this area (Iceland).
- For countries with moderate/high adjustment needs, and where structural expenditure has risen rapidly during the crisis and is at a medium to high level, the strategy should focus on expenditure reductions (Australia, Belgium, Canada, Finland, Netherlands, Poland, and South Africa). This is particularly the case where the desire or options for increases in taxes are limited. For others, possibilities for efficiency-enhancing revenue measures, including through administration reforms, should be fully explored (Austria, Germany, and Italy). In addition, where there is scope for significantly improving revenues, reforms should include measures in this area, as well as a reversal of stimulus spending (China).

Table 1.2. Selected Advanced and Emerging Economies: Adjustment Strategy and Illustrative Adjustment Needs

	More Reliance on Tax	*Tax and Expenditure*	*More Reliance on Expenditure*
High adjustment *(>6 percent of GDP)*		France, India, Ireland, Japan, Portugal, Spain, the United Kingdom, and the United States	Poland
Moderate adjustment *(Between 3 and 6 percent of GDP)*		Austria, China, Germany, and Italy	Australia, Belgium, Canada, Finland, the Netherlands, and South Africa
Low adjustment *(<3 percent of GDP)*	Indonesia Mexico	Iceland	Argentina, Brazil, Russia, Saudi Arabia, Sweden, and Turkey

Note: Adjustment needs are defined as in Figure 1.1, horizontal axis. Therefore, they exclude the measures needed to offset age-related spending increases.

- Some countries with high adjustment needs will require measures on both sides. This includes France, Greece, India, Ireland, Japan, Portugal, Spain, the United Kingdom, and the United States.
- All countries will need to develop a strategy to deal with age-related expenditures. For advanced countries where spending pressures are higher, a reasonable goal would be to keep these outlays constant (relative to GDP) over the medium term. For emerging market economies, the focus would be on improving the efficiency of this spending and program design at an early stage, to ensure that the expansion of coverage over the longer term is fiscally sustainable.

CHAPTER

2 Expenditure Reform

Expenditure Reform: Key Principles

Expenditure reforms should be guided by two objectives:

- *Improving the efficiency of spending.* Countries should seek to reduce the cost of producing existing public sector outputs. In addition, spending should be allocated to activities that provide the greatest marginal benefits to society as a whole; and
- *Ensuring equity.* Growth without equity is less durable (Berg, Ostry, and Zettelmeyer, 2008; and Tanzi, Chu, and Gupta, 1999). Expenditure policy must reflect the need for both intra- and intergenerational equity. In view of demographic pressures, ensuring intergenerational equity will require altering the terms of social insurance in many countries. Greater targeting of social spending may also be necessary to ensure that the poor are protected as spending levels are reduced as a share of GDP.

Expenditure Structure and Trends

Cross-country differences in the size and composition of government spending are sizeable, reflecting differences in the level of development, role of the state, and spending efficiency. Expenditure is generally higher in advanced economies, reflecting more expansive social benefits (Tables 2.1a and 2.1b). There are also significant variations within the advanced economies, reflecting differences in demographic structure and socio-political preferences regarding the role of government. Outlays for the wage bill are higher in advanced than emerging economies. Capital expenditures are generally higher in emerging economies, but with wide variation across

Table 2.1a. Expenditure Structure: Advanced Economies, 2008

	(In percent of GDP)					*(In percent of primary expenditure)*			
	Primary expenditure	Compensation of employees	Social benefits	Capital spending	Other	Compensation of employees	Social benefits	Capital spending	Other
Australia [1,2]	30.4	8.8	9.6	2.6	9.4	28.9	31.6	8.6	30.9
Austria [3]	46.3	9.2	23.6	1.1	12.4	19.9	51.0	2.4	26.8
Belgium [3]	46.2	12.1	23.3	1.7	9.1	26.2	50.4	3.7	19.7
Canada [4]	36.1	11.6	7.5	1.4	15.6	32.1	20.7	3.9	43.3
Cyprus [3]	39.8	14.1	12.1	3.0	10.6	35.4	30.4	7.5	26.6
Czech Rep. [4]	41.8	7.6	18.2	5.0	11.0	18.2	43.5	12.0	26.3
Denmark [3]	50.5	17.3	16.4	1.8	15.0	34.3	32.5	3.6	29.7
Finland [3]	47.5	13.4	17.7	2.6	13.8	28.2	37.3	5.5	29.1
France [3]	49.9	12.7	23.3	3.2	10.7	25.5	46.7	6.4	21.4
Germany [3]	41.0	6.9	24.3	1.5	8.3	16.8	59.3	3.7	20.2
Greece [3]	43.7	11.5	19.1	2.9	10.2	26.3	43.7	6.6	23.3
Hong Kong [1,2]	16.7	4.2	4.4	0.0	8.1	25.0	26.2	0.0	48.7
Iceland [3]	54.4	14.6	6.1	4.5	29.2	26.8	11.2	8.3	53.7
Ireland [3]	41.0	11.1	13.8	5.3	10.8	27.1	33.7	12.9	26.3
Israel [2]	40.2	12.1	9.3	0.1	18.7	30.1	23.2	0.2	46.5
Italy [3]	43.6	10.9	20.4	2.2	10.1	25.0	46.8	5.0	23.2
Japan [5,6]	33.5	6.2	17.7	3.6	6.0	18.4	52.9	10.8	18.0
Korea [5,6]	29.1	7.3	5.9	5.7	10.2	25.1	20.1	19.6	35.2
Luxembourg [3]	37.4	7.1	18.1	3.6	8.6	19.0	48.4	9.6	23.0
Malta [3]	41.7	14.6	13.3	2.5	11.3	35.0	31.9	6.0	27.1
Netherlands [3]	43.8	9.1	20.2	3.5	11.0	20.8	46.1	8.0	25.1
New Zealand [6,7]	38.1	9.3	13.3	3.3	12.1	24.4	35.0	8.7	31.8
Norway [3]	38.5	12.0	13.6	3.1	9.8	31.2	35.3	8.1	25.5
Portugal [3]	43.0	12.9	19.9	2.2	8.0	30.0	46.3	5.1	18.6
Singapore [1,2]	14.6	4.2	3.1	1.5	5.8	28.9	21.5	10.3	39.4
Slovak Rep. [3]	33.6	6.6	15.6	2.0	9.4	19.6	46.4	6.0	28.0
Slovenia [3]	43.1	11.1	16.7	4.3	11.0	25.8	38.7	10.0	25.5
Spain [3]	39.5	10.8	15.0	3.8	9.9	27.3	38.0	9.6	25.1
Sweden [3]	51.3	14.9	18.2	3.3	14.9	29.0	35.5	6.4	29.0
Switzerland [1,3]	31.0	7.7	11.6	1.9	9.8	24.8	37.4	6.1	31.6
United Kingdon	45.0	11.0	13.1	2.3	18.6	24.4	29.1	5.1	41.3
United States [4]	36.1	10.2	12.9	1.0	12.0	28.2	35.7	2.9	33.3
Average	38.1	9.6	15.3	2.1	11.1	25.3	39.6	5.7	29.3
Advanced G-20	37.7	9.5	15.2	2.0	11.1	25.2	39.8	5.5	29.6

Sources: WEO; Eurostat; Government Finance Statistics (GFS); and OECD.

[1]2007 data.

[2]GFS.

[3]Eurostat; capital spending proxied by "gross fixed capital formation."

[4]WEO.

[5]2006 data.

[6]OECD; capital spending proxied by "gross fixed capital formation."

[7]2005 data.

Table 2.1b. Expenditure Structure: Emerging Market Economies, 2008

	(In percent of GDP)					*(In percent of primary expenditure)*			
	Primary expenditure	Compensation of employees	Social benefits	Capital spending	Other	Compensation of employees	Social benefits	Capital spending	Other
Argentina [1 2]	30.4	10.1	12.6	3.8	3.9	33.3	...	12.6	...
Brazil [1 2]	32.5	9.7	12.7	2.6	7.5	29.9	...	8.0	...
Bulgaria [3]	36.5	9.0	12.0	5.7	9.8	24.7	32.9	15.6	26.8
Chile [1 4]	22.6	5.3	4.6	4.1	8.6	23.6	20.3	17.9	38.1
China [1]	20.5	...	...	...	...	...	...	...	...
Colombia [1]	23.0	5.6	7.5	5.1	4.9	24.2	32.5	21.9	21.3
Croatia [5 6]	40.2	9.9	15.5	4.2	10.6	24.6	38.6	10.4	26.4
Egypt [6]	31.0	7.1	4.0	5.2	14.6	22.9	13.0	16.8	47.3
Hungary [3]	45.1	11.5	18.7	2.8	12.1	25.5	41.5	6.2	26.8
India [1 2]	23.6	...	4.1	...	...	...	...	...	...
Indonesia [1 7]	18.6	4.6	0.8	5.7	7.5	24.9	...	30.5	...
Malaysia [1 2]	27.3	...	6.5	3.0	...	...	...	11.0	...
Mexico [1 8]	22.2	5.9	7.4	5.5	3.4	26.6	...	24.8	...
Nigeria [1]	28.2	...	...	...	...	...	...	...	...
Pakistan [1 2]	17.4	...	1.9	...	...	...	...	...	...
Peru [1]	17.3	5.1	2.3	3.8	6.0	29.7	13.3	22.2	34.8
Philippines [1 2]	13.1	5.0	3.1	2.4	2.7	38.1	...	18.1	...
Poland [3]	41.1	10.0	16.2	4.6	10.3	24.3	39.4	11.2	25.1
Romania [3]	37.6	10.2	11.2	5.6	10.6	27.1	29.8	14.9	28.2
Russia [1]	34.0	7.6	9.4	6.5	10.5	22.3	27.6	19.2	31.0
Saudi Arabia [1 8]	29.9	10.6	2.2	7.4	9.7	35.6	...	24.6	...
South Africa [1]	27.4	9.7	10.7	1.9	5.1	35.4	39.0	7.1	18.5
Turkey [1]	28.4	6.9	10.5	3.8	7.2	24.3	37.1	13.3	25.3
Ukraine [6]	46.5	10.6	19.5	5.7	10.7	22.7	41.9	12.3	23.1
Average	25.8	7.9	10.7	4.7	7.7	26.9	22.7	16.8	21.0
Emerging G-20	24.8	7.9	10.8	4.8	7.3	27.3	20.4	17.5	18.1

Sources: WEO; Eurostat; GFS; ILO; and IMF staff estimates.
[1]WEO.
[2]ILO Social Security Department database Global Extension of Social Security (GESS), accessible at http://www.socialsecurityextension.org/gimi/gess/ShowTheme.do?tid=1985.
[3]Eurostat; capital spending proxied by "gross fixed capital formation."
[4]"Social benefits" include social security benefits only.
[5]2007 data.
[6]GFS.
[7]Public pensions only.
[8]IMF staff estimates.

Figure 2.1. Age-Related Expenditure Trends in the Advanced Economies
(In percent of GDP)

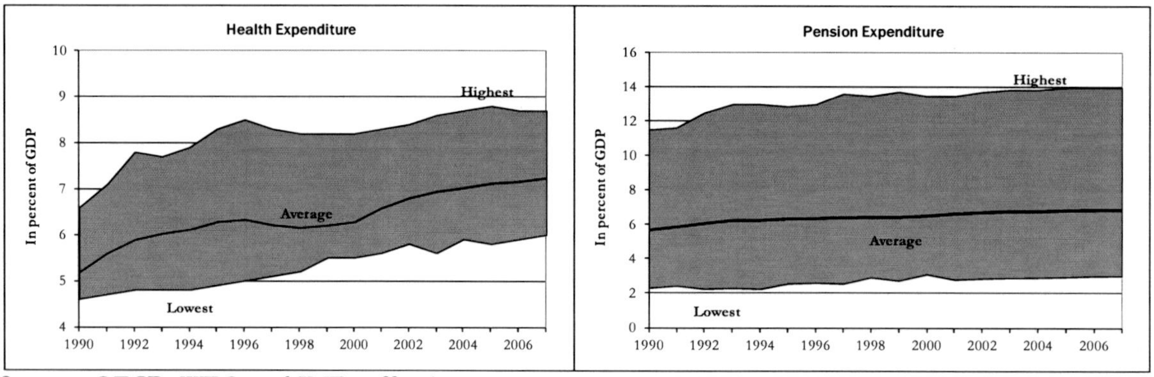

Sources: OECD; WEO; and IMF staff estimates.
Note: Countries included in the sample are Australia, Canada, France, Germany, Italy, Japan, the United Kingdom, and the United States.

countries. Although high spending alone does not indicate inefficiency, several studies suggest that many countries could achieve similar levels of public services in education and health at a lower cost (Carcillo, Gunnarsson, and Verhoeven, 2007; and Afonso, Schuknecht, and Tanzi, 2005 and 2006).

Age-related spending has been the main driver of current spending over the past two decades. Within the advanced countries, age-related outlays have risen since 1990 by roughly 2 percentage points of GDP (Figure 2.1). Increases have been especially large for pensions in Japan and Korea in the past decade, and for health spending in Korea (from a low level) and France, Greece, and Portugal. Demographics have been an important catalyst behind these increases, particularly in pensions, in the advanced economies. For health, technology[4] and its interaction with an ageing population have been the key drivers behind rising spending. These trends are expected to continue in the coming years for both advanced and emerging economies (see discussion below on age-related spending).

Reinforcing past trends, primary current expenditures, adjusted for the cycle, have risen further during the crisis. After the success of the 1990s in containing spending increases as a percent of GDP—owing to reductions in non-age-related outlays—primary current spending began drifting upward in the years prior to the crisis, but with wide variation across countries (Figures 2.1 and 2.2; and Figures A.1 and A.2). In some countries with moderate and

[4]The term "technology" captures the effect of medical innovations and factors that have in the past provided improved health care, but at higher relative prices.

Figure 2.2. Primary Expenditure Trends in the Advanced Economies
(In percent of GDP)

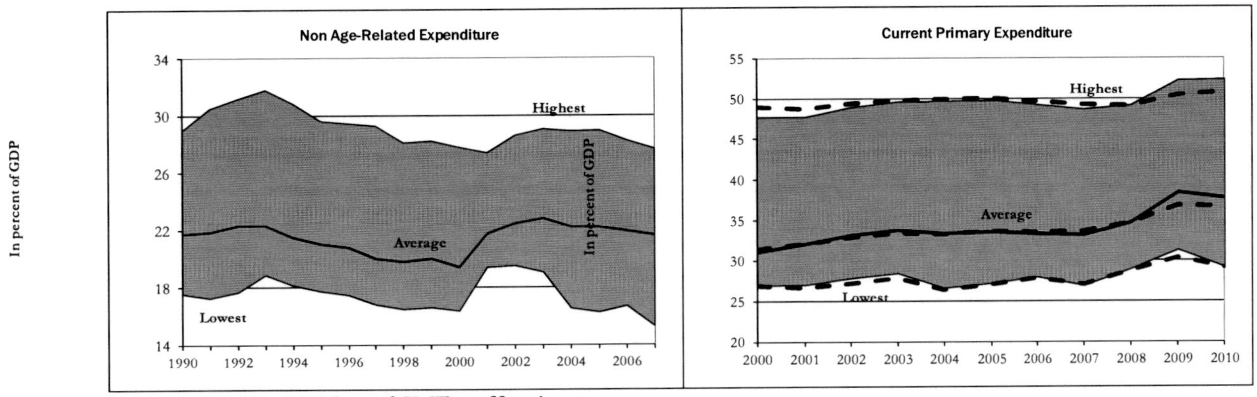

Sources: OECD; WEO; and IMF staff estimates.
Notes: Countries included in the sample are Australia, Canada, France, Germany, Italy, Japan, the United Kingdom, and the United States; and the dashed line represents percent of potential GDP.

high adjustment needs, current primary spending was already rising in 2000–07, including for wages (Italy, the United Kingdom, and the United States). Primary current spending also increased steadily in many emerging economies such as Argentina, Brazil, Mexico, and South Africa (Figure A.3). Since the crisis, current outlays have accounted for the bulk of the rise in spending in the advanced G-20, partly reflecting safety net spending. Of the increase in structural spending of about 2½–3 percentage points of GDP in the advanced G-20 economies between 2007 and 2010, about 1½ percentage point can be attributed to discretionary stimulus measures. In the emerging G-20, primary balances have weakened due to higher spending, especially for social benefits, the wage bill, and public investment.

Expenditure Reform Strategy

In countries requiring fiscal consolidation, the adjustment on the spending side will have to go well beyond the expiration of the stimulus spending increases; more fundamental reforms are needed. Non-renewal of the stimulus spending would lower spending by 1½ percent of GDP in the advanced and emerging G-20 economies, only a fraction of the needed adjustment.

A two pillar strategy could anchor expenditure reform, guided by the following objectives (Ali Abbas and others, 2010):

- *Stabilize age-related spending relative to GDP.* Given the major trend increase in these outlays, reducing this spending would be difficult. The goal should thus be to stabilize spending-to-GDP ratios, which will require significant structural reform.

- *Reduce non-age-related spending relative to GDP.* A possible policy goal would be to stabilize aggregate non-age-related spending in real per capita terms so that the ratio of GDP drops as growth picks up. In the advanced economies, for example, freezing non-age-related spending in real per capita terms over the next 10 years—beyond the savings arising from the non-renewal of stimulus spending—could generate structural savings of about 3–3½ percentage points of GDP.[5] Similar policies helped underpin some successful fiscal consolidations in the 1980s and 1990s, such as in Belgium (1983–89), Denmark (1982–86), Finland (1993–2000), Israel (1980–83), and Sweden (1993–2000).

To achieve these goals, medium-term expenditure reforms will need to improve the composition and efficiency of expenditure. The freeze in real spending is an overall policy goal, not a tool. Targeted structural reforms would be needed to achieve this goal. In both advanced and emerging economies, reforms in wages, subsidies, and transfers have been the most durable and conducive to economic growth.[6] Staff analysis of the experience with large fiscal adjustments provides a similar picture, with cuts in the wage bill comprising about a quarter of the adjustment and social benefits and transfers accounting for almost a third (Table A.1). Containing age-related spending has also been an important element of the adjustment.[7] A breakdown by functional classification shows that reductions in general public services, economic affairs, and defense spending have comprised an important element of adjustments among advanced economies in these episodes (Table A.2).

Better targeting of social welfare spending, including social benefits, could provide substantial fiscal savings. Social benefits are large—both in percent of GDP and as a share of spending—in many countries with high adjustment needs (Tables 2.1a and 2.1b).[8] Much of this spending, however, is not well

[5]The spending to GDP ratio would decline faster as GDP moves back to potential. This projection is based on an assumption of a 2 percent potential growth rate.

[6]See, for example, Gupta and others (2005), Hauptmeier, Heipertz, and Schuknecht (2006), and Kumar, Leigh, and Plekhanov (2007).

[7]In light of the increasing trend in age-related spending, the size of adjustment in past successful consolidation episodes has been larger than that suggested by Table A.1.

[8]Even after excluding health services and pensions, gross social spending is sizeable (around 6½ percent of GDP in the OECD in 2005; unweighted).

targeted. In the OECD, less than 10 percent of public social spending is means-tested (Adema and Ladaique, 2009). This partly reflects a high share of age-related, insurance-based outlays in social spending. Nonetheless, the effectiveness of cash transfers in reducing inequality varies considerably, even among countries with similar systems (ILO, 2010, OECD, 2008a). In the European Union, less than a third of non-age-related benefits are means-tested (Figure 2.3). This suggests substantial scope to reduce these outlays without sacrificing equity objectives. Improved targeting of tax benefits (including for employer-provided benefits) should also be explored, with due consideration of the implied increase in marginal tax rates (see also discussion in Chapter 3 on personal income taxes).

The design of unemployment benefits could be improved. As employment recovers, spending programs providing long-term assistance to the unemployed should be reexamined. The high long-term replacement rates of unemployment benefits in some countries, for example, can have high fiscal costs and adverse labor market effects (OECD, 2009b) (Figure 2.4). Staff estimates that in countries with above-average replacement rates, reducing them to the OECD average could yield savings of almost ½ percent of GDP. Efforts to tighten the duration and generosity of out-of-work benefits, with increased emphasis on in-work benefits as well as a tightening of eligibility for sickness and disability benefits, would minimize disincentives for labor force participation (Carcillo and Grubb, 2006). These policies will be all the more important in the context of declining labor supply due to ageing populations.

Reversing recent increases in military expenditure could also yield savings. Reducing outlays in the advanced economies to pre-crisis levels could generate savings of about ½ percent of GDP (Figure 2.5). Returning spending to levels prevailing roughly a decade ago would yield 1 percent of GDP.

Sizable savings are possible in spending on subsidies. Subsidies averaged about 1 percent of GDP in 2007 in OECD countries, and equaled or exceeded 2 percent of GDP in Austria, Belgium, Denmark, and Switzerland. This spending, including for agricultural subsidies—which are large in some countries—should be reexamined and replaced, where possible, with more targeted instruments to provide income support. In particular, priority should be given to phasing out energy subsidies, including for petroleum products. Tax-inclusive subsidies for these products, which also incorporate estimates of the needed taxation to offset externalities, are projected to reach 1 percent

Figure 2.3. Targeting of Non-Age-Related Social Spending, 2007

(In percent of GDP)

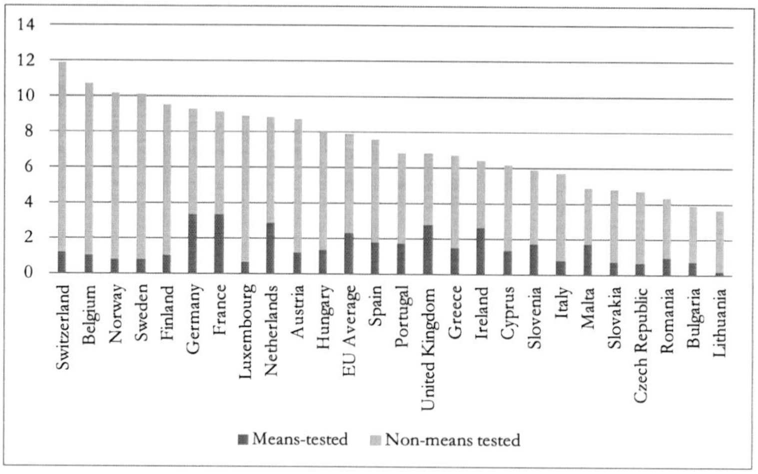

Source: Eurostat.

Note: Non-age-related social spending reflects social benefits excluding old-age and health spending.

Figure 2.4. Generosity of Long-Term Unemployment Benefits

(In percent)

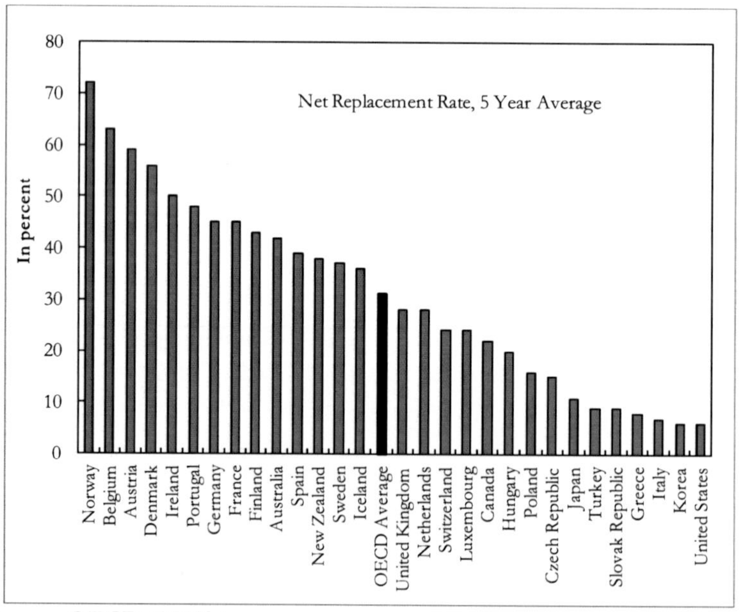

Source: OECD (2009b).

Note: Unweighted averages, for earnings levels of 67 percent and 100 percent of average wage and four family types. Includes cash incomes, income taxes, and social security contributions. Excludes social assistance or housing related benefits. For further details see www.oecd.org/els/social/workincentives.

Figure 2.5. Military Expenditure in Advanced Economies, 1990–2010

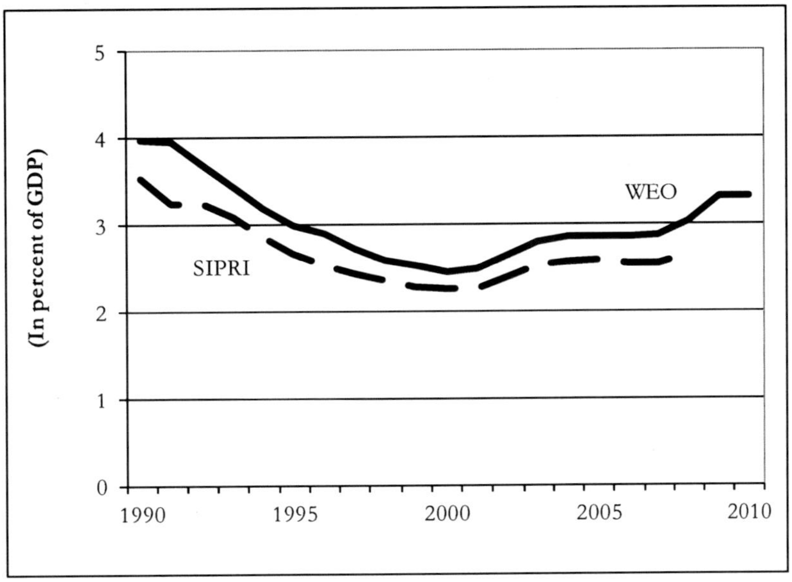

Sources: Stockholm International Peace Research Institute (SIPRI) military expenditure database; and WEO.

of global GDP in 2010 (Coady and others, 2010) (see also below). Advanced economies account for about a quarter of this total, and emerging countries over half.

Public spending on climate change is expected to increase, but this can be moderated by improving the efficiency of these outlays.[9] Subsidies for renewable electricity and biofuels may have become excessive.[10] Potentially more productive spending to address climate change includes programs for energy R&D and low-carbon or climate-resilient infrastructure. While additional expenditures (in some cases substantial) are needed to address climate concerns in advanced and emerging countries, the primary focus of climate policies should be to reduce emissions through the appropriate carbon pricing (see below). Even beyond countries' domestic climate policies, increased public expenditures from advanced countries will be needed to help meet commitments to support adaptation and mitigation in developing countries (pledged to reach $100 billion by 2020).

[9]For additional discussion, see IMF (2008a), and Jones and Keen (2009).

[10]Tax credits to biofuels in the United States, for example, could exceed US$19 billion a year by 2022.

Expenditure reviews could help guide the design of country-specific strategies. These reviews, which have played a key role in expenditure reform in several advanced economies, can provide valuable input to guide long-term reform by addressing fundamental questions on the role of government and the cost effectiveness of different policy interventions (IMF, 2008b; and Kelly, 2007). These reviews should also identify expenditure inefficiencies and be integrated with performance-based budgeting.

Coordination with subnational government will be crucial for ensuring successful expenditure reform. Subnational governments often account for a sizeable share of the adjustment during successful fiscal consolidations (Darby, Muscatelli, and Roy, 2004; and Kumar, Leigh, and Plekhanov, 2007). Clarifying expenditure responsibilities and revenue assignments has helped strengthen budget constraints on local governments, while negotiation of binding fiscal targets has helped to coordinate policies across the different tiers of government. Use of cooperative arrangements between different levels of government also helps increase ownership of shared economic and fiscal objectives (IMF, 2009).

Age-Related Spending

Significant challenges lie ahead in dealing with age-related spending, especially health care. Public expenditure on pensions is projected to rise by 1 percentage point of GDP between 2010 and 2030 in the advanced economies. The relatively modest increase in this spending—in spite of the ageing of the population—reflects the significant reforms that have already been made in many countries. A further deepening of these reforms could place public pension spending on a sustainable path. In health, in contrast, the outlook is more challenging. Staff projects an increase in spending of about 3½ percentage points of GDP over the next 20 years. Containing the growth of public expenditures on health care will thus need to figure prominently in fiscal consolidation strategies over the next several years.

Pension systems

Staff projects that pension spending will increase by an average of 1 percentage point of GDP over the next 20 years (Appendix 3 and Figure 2.6). Large increases in pension expenditures are projected in advanced countries that have not substantially reformed their traditional pay-as-you-go systems (especially in Belgium, Greece, and Luxembourg). In other advanced economies, the increase in pension expenditures would be less marked due to

Figure 2.6. Change in Public Pension Expenditures, 2010–30
(In percent of GDP)

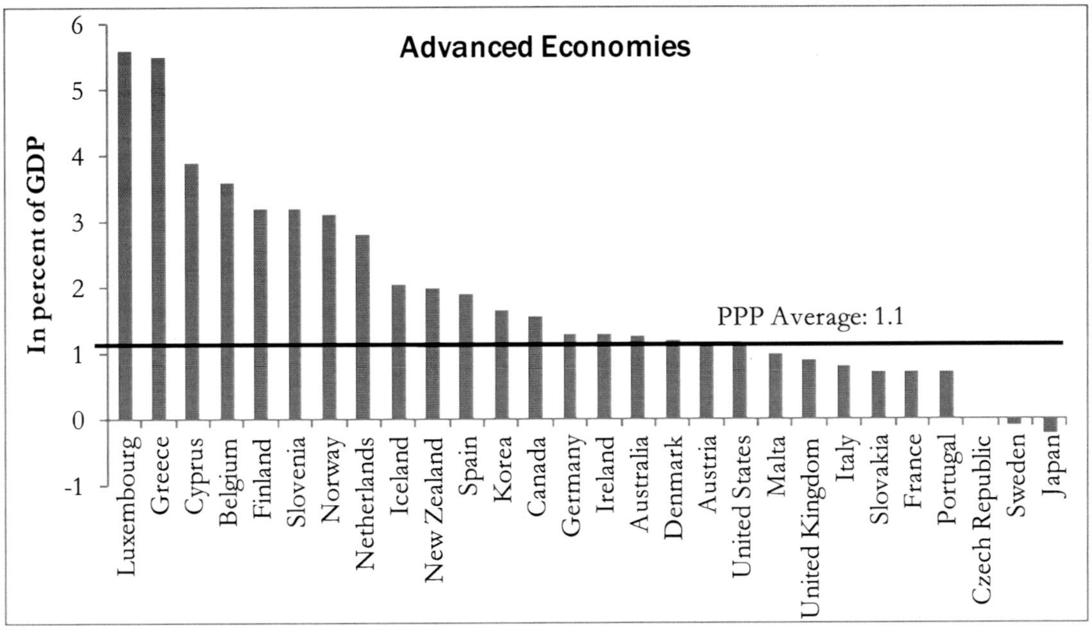

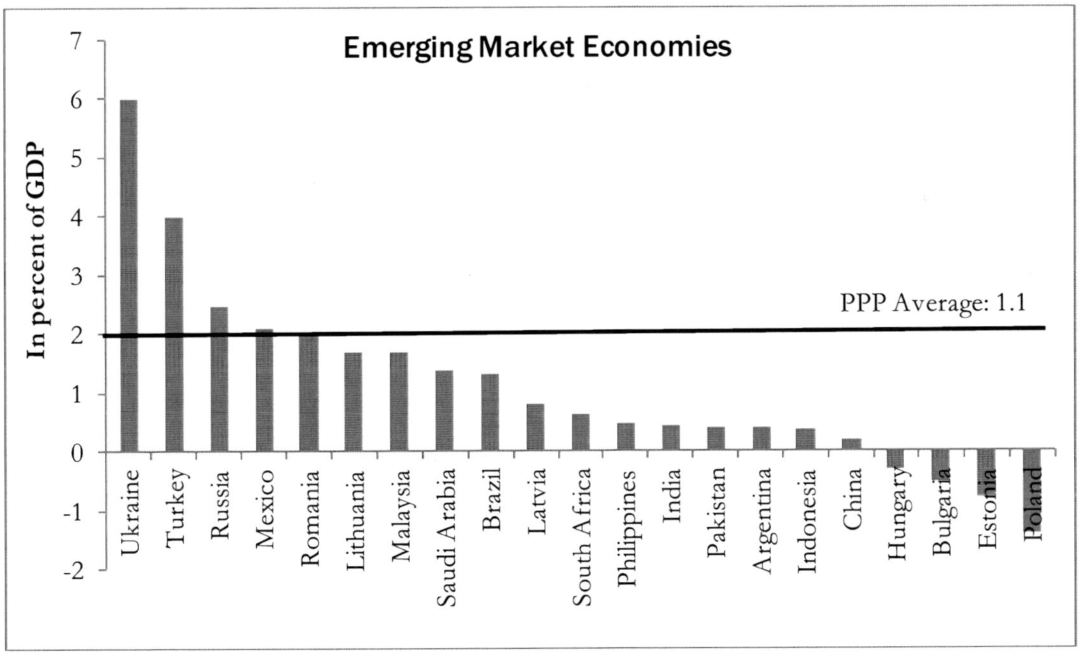

Sources: Country authorities; EC (2009); OECD (2009); ILO (2010); and IMF staff estimates.

Table 2.2. Net Present Value of Future Pension Spending Increases
(In percent of GDP)

	2011-2030	2031-2050	2010-onwards
Average	8.3	23.2	153.5
Advanced	8.7	21.5	138.4
Emerging	7.8	25.9	177.1
G20	7.7	20.4	129.6
Advanced	7.3	16.7	100.3
Emerging	7.2	26.1	174.3

Source: IMF staff estimates.

the projected impact of already legislated reforms in offsetting the demographic pressures (Appendices 4 and 5).[11] Adjustment needs may well be larger, though, as the projections assume that these reforms will not be reversed, even when they involve large cuts in replacement rates (as in Italy and Japan). Among the emerging economies, those with relatively high spending in 2010 are projected to experience the steepest increase in pension expenditures (especially Russia and Ukraine) over the next 20 years. In several other emerging countries, where coverage is currently low, the projected increase in expenditures is much less severe (China, India, and Pakistan).[12] Beyond 2030, emerging economies are expected to experience a faster pace of ageing compared to the advanced economies.

The cumulative fiscal cost of future pension spending increases is large (Table 2.2). Over the next 20 years, the net present value (NPV) of pension spending increases is about 8½ percent of GDP for advanced economies and 8 percent of GDP for emerging countries. The fiscal cost of pension increases over the subsequent 20 years is even larger—over 20 percent of GDP for both advanced countries and emerging economies.[13]

[11]In some countries, projected increases are modest, reflecting the limited role played by public pensions. Within the G-20, Australia and Mexico have added a mandatory, private, defined-contribution component to the pension system. Private, funded pensions are also significant in Canada, the United Kingdom, and the United States.

[12]These projections should be interpreted as lower-bound estimates for emerging economies, as they do not incorporate the impact of the likely expansion of pension coverage to a larger share of the population. See Table A.3 for projections by country.

[13]The calculation uses a discount rate of 1 percent a year in excess of GDP growth. See Table A.3 for more details.

Figure 2.7. Illustration of Policy Options to Offset a Pension Spending Increase of 1 Percentage Point of GDP

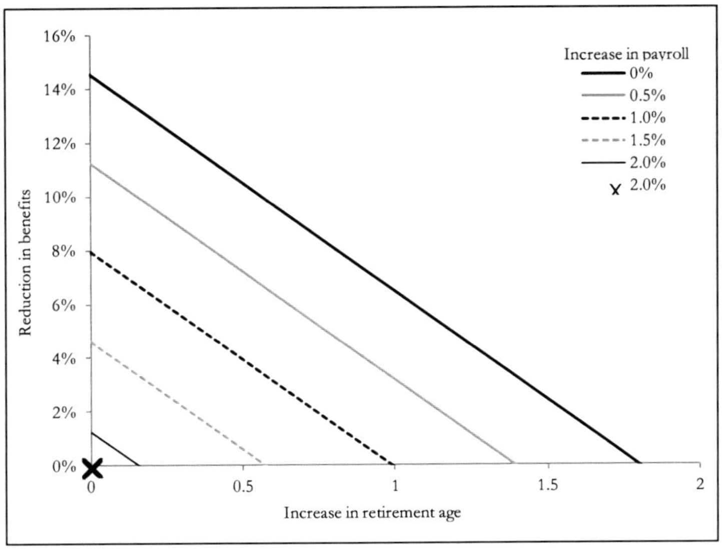

Source: IMF staff estimates.

Advanced and emerging economies face different challenges. In countries where coverage is extensive, the share of elderly population is larger, and spending is high—mainly the advanced countries—the primary objective should be to stabilize pension expenditures over the longer term while maintaining a reasonable rate of return on pension contributions and ensuring that pension benefits are adequate to prevent old-age poverty. In contrast, in the emerging economies, which generally have lower expenditures due to younger populations and less extensive coverage, the challenge is to expand pension coverage, but in a manner that does not generate fiscal imbalances as these systems mature.[14] For emerging economies with high household savings rates (such as China), increased pension coverage would also support efforts to make domestic demand the primary catalyst of growth (see Baldacci and others, 2010).

Three policy options are available to offset the projected increase in spending of 1 percentage point of GDP between 2010 and 2030.[15] Figure 2.7 illustrates the tradeoffs across the typical options available to offset increases in pension spending—raising the statutory retirement age, reducing benefits, or

[14]See World Bank and OECD (2009).

[15]Pension reform can also have positive macroeconomic effects. See Disney (2005), Nickel, Rother, and Theophilopoulou (2008), and Karam and others (forthcoming).

increasing contribution rates. A two-year increase in the statutory retirement age would be sufficient to stabilize pension spending as a share of GDP at its 2010 level over the next two decades. This two-year increase in statutory retirement ages is roughly equivalent to a cut in benefits of 15 percent (corners of black solid line) and delivers similar fiscal effects as a 2 percentage-point increase in payroll taxes (origin).[16]

Raising statutory retirement ages should be the starting point for reform. Raising retirement ages would have a powerful effect: a one-year increase in the statutory age in the advanced countries would offset about half of the increase in spending projected between 2010 and 2030.[17] Increases in statutory retirement ages are largely justified by the projected increase in longevity over the next 20 years: between 2010 and 2030, the number of years individuals are expected to live beyond the statutory retirement age is projected to increase by an average of 2 years in emerging and advanced countries (Table 2.3). Increases in the statutory retirement age should be accompanied by steps to limit the generosity of early retirement programs, which allow individuals to claim pensions, on average, by about 4 years earlier than the statutory age. It will also be important to tighten eligibility for disability pensions.

Raising the statutory retirement age, however, may not be sufficient in some countries to offset the projected increases in pension spending. The remainder of the increase in expenditures could be addressed with a combination of benefit reductions and increases in contributions.

- *Reduce benefits.* Many advanced countries have already moved in this direction—in Japan, Korea, and Sweden, benefit cuts of nearly 20 percent or more are set to occur within the next 20 years (Table 2.4). Benefits could be reduced by modifying the base used to calculate benefits, modifying indexation rules, or taxing pensions.[18] Cuts in pensions, however, should preserve benefits that are sufficient to lift the

[16]The estimates assume that only half of the affected "retirees" continue to work. See Barrell, Hurst, and Kirby (2009) for a similar analysis that takes into account the macroeconomic effects of increasing effective retirement ages.

[17]This increase in statutory retirement ages would need to be on top of already scheduled increases to achieve fiscal savings. To keep pension spending from rising after 2030, additional reforms would be needed. This could be either through a further increase in the retirement age of about 9 months, a benefit cut of 5.3 percent, or an increase in contribution rates of about 0.90 percentage points.

[18]See Piggott and Sane (2009) for a discussion of the different types of indexation rules and their effects on financial sustainability, equity, and efficiency.

Table 2.3. Statutory Retirement Ages and Years in Retirement

	Earliest eligibility age for pension benefits, 2010	Statutory retirement age, 2010	Life expectancy at statutory retirement age, 2010	Life expectancy at statutory retirement age, 2030
Average	58.9	63.0	17.9	19.9
Advanced	60.1	64.2	17.7	19.7
Emerging	57.1	61.2	18.2	20.3
G-20	57.8	62.4	18.2	20.0
Advanced G-20	60.4	64.0	18.5	20.3
Emerging G-20	55.4	60.9	17.9	19.7

Source: IMF staff estimates.
Notes: Legislated and planned increases in statutory retirement ages are included in the calculations for 2030. See Table A.4 for figures by country.

Table 2.4. Tax Wedge and Replacement Rates

	Social security contribution rate (in percent of labor cost)	Total tax wedge (in percent of labor cost)	Replacement rates		
			2010	2030	Percent change, 2010-2030
Australia	5.7	26.9	23.1	23.1	0
Austria	36.5	48.8	54.2	54.2	0
Belgium	34.2	56.0	46.5	47.9	3
Canada	16.8	31.3	44.5	...	...
Czech Republic	35.2	43.4	41.6	35.4	-15
Denmark	11.0	41.2	39.4	38.3	-3
Finland	24.3	43.5	51.2	51.7	1
France	39.4	49.3	63.3	52.9	-16
Germany	33.4	52.0	50.4	45.9	-9
Greece	34.4	42.4	72.2	85.9	19
Hungary	38.3	54.1	42.3	38.8	-8
Iceland	5.2	28.3	52.8	52.8	0
Ireland	14.4	22.9	28.5	30.4	7
Italy	31.5	46.5	71.3	64.1	-10
Japan	22.4	29.5	40.6	33.9	-17
Korea	15.8	20.3	57.8	46.2	-20
Luxembourg	22.5	35.9	41.4	39.3	-5
Netherlands	31.2	45.0	41.8	40.4	-3
New Zealand	0.0	21.2	41.1	41.1	0
Norway	18.3	37.7	56.2	53.3	-5
Poland	33.7	39.7	59.6	45.1	-24
Portugal	28.1	37.6	49.0	42.3	-14
Slovak Republic	31.4	38.9	45.8	41.0	-10
Spain	28.0	37.8	62.6	61.0	-3
Sweden	29.8	44.6	48.1	36.6	-24
Turkey	29.3	39.7	86.9	69.5	-20
United Kingdom	18.0	32.8	34.6	34.5	0
United States	14.3	30.1	38.7	35.0	-10
Average	24.4	38.5	49.5	45.9	-7

Sources: OECD (2009a); and IMF staff estimates.

elderly out of poverty. Consideration should also be given to rules that link benefits and contributions to demographic and economic variables to maintain actuarial balance.[19] Additionally, economies looking to expand coverage while containing the growth of expenditures might consider means testing of pensions (as in Australia, and to some degree Canada).[20] Means testing, however, could weaken the link between contributions and benefits, hampering efforts to increase compliance and expand coverage.

- *Increase contributions.* Changes in rates of social contributions need to be assessed together with potential changes in the rate of personal tax on labor income (discussed in Chapter 3), since it is their combination that determines the effective marginal and average tax rates likely to affect labor participation and hours worked decisions.[21] Taxes on earnings are already high in a number of countries (in Austria, Belgium, France, Germany, Hungary, and Italy, the tax wedge is already near or above 50 percent of total labor costs). Other countries may have room for raising payroll contribution rates (Australia, Iceland, Ireland, Japan, Korea, New Zealand, and the United States have a tax wedge at or below 30 percent), and in some cases it may be appropriate to lift the ceiling on earnings subject to contributions. The incentive effects of social contributions, however, might be less marked if their payment is seen (correctly or not) as implying increased benefit entitlement.

Health care

Concerns about the sustainability of publicly-financed health systems have featured prominently in the United States, but much less in Europe; however, the outlook is grim also for Europe. Differences in assumptions about whether or not technological change will continue to drive up the cost of health care explain much of the differences in available projections for the United States and Europe. For the United States, the Congressional Budget

[19]In Japan, "macro indexing" is achieved by reducing pensionable earnings (for future beneficiaries) and benefits (for current beneficiaries) by the rate of decrease in the number of contributors and increase in life expectancy at age 65. In Canada, benefits are required to be reduced, or contributions increased, to address long-term actuarial imbalances. Other countries use notional defined contribution arrangements, which connect contributions to benefits, to respond to economic and demographic developments. In Italy, for example, notional balances grow in line with GDP growth; in Sweden, notional returns are based on the rate of growth of economy-wide earnings.

[20]In Australia, an income test applies to the "Age Pension" system; in Canada, the income test applies to the old age security pension and the guaranteed income supplement.

[21]Gruber and Wise (2002); Voňková and van Soest (2009); and Liebman, Luttner, and Seif (2008).

Office (2007) projects an increase in health spending of 3.7 percentage points of GDP over the next two decades, based on the assumption that the increased spending per-capita arises from better, but also more expensive, medical services due to continued technological progress. In contrast, the European Commission's Ageing Report (European Commission, 2009)—widely used for international comparisons—projects an increase in health spending of 0.7 percentage point of GDP, using a baseline assumption of no further increase in per capita spending due to technological progress. While much uncertainty exists, this is an extreme assumption that appears unrealistic based on historic trends.

Under the assumption that relative prices for health services will continue to rise in line with recent trends, staff projects that public spending on health will also continue to rise at a fast pace in both advanced and emerging economies. Public expenditures on health care are forecast to increase by over 3½ percentage points of GDP by 2030 in advanced countries, to 10½ percent of GDP on average (Figure 2.8).[22] In emerging economies, the projected increase amounts to 1 percentage point of GDP, reaching 4 percent of GDP. In more than half of countries, public health spending would exceed 8 percent of GDP by 2030 (Table A.5). France, Germany, and the United States are projected to experience the largest increases of at least 3½ percentage points of GDP, while the smallest increases would be in India and Pakistan (less than ½ percentage point).

Ageing and other non-demographic factors will also contribute, albeit to a lesser extent than technology. These include income growth, the expansion of insurance, and provider reimbursement methods (Gerdtham and Jonsson, 2000; and Smith, Newhouse, and Freeland, 2009).[23] In contrast to pensions, demographic change alone accounts for a relatively modest share of the projected increases in health spending (Figure 2.8). The relatively high increase in health spending—compared to pensions—also reflects the fact that the pension projections incorporate reforms that have already been agreed in legislation, which will help offset the effects of ageing. In health, in

---

[22]Projections for health spending under different assumptions for excess cost growth (relative to GDP per capita) are presented in Table A.5.

[23]Technology and other non-demographic factors have also interacted with an ageing population to drive up expenditure over time. That is, because health expenditures are higher for older cohorts, over time the effect of technology and non-demographic changes are magnified.

Figure 2.8. Increase in Public Health Spending in Baseline Scenario
(In percent of GDP)

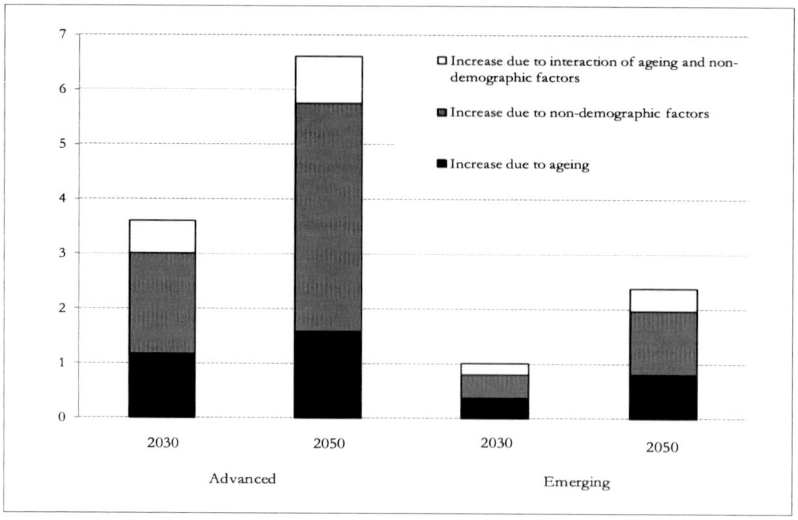

Sources: IMF staff estimates; and sources listed in Appendix 6.

contrast, no major reforms have been agreed, or they are too uncertain to incorporate into the projections.[24]

The principal policy challenges differ in advanced and most emerging economies. In advanced economies, public health care systems are well developed, and the top priority is to contain the high rates of spending growth that have led to marked increases in spending-to-GDP ratios over the past 50 years (Table 2.5). In emerging economies, in contrast, the challenge is to expand basic coverage to a larger share of the population at a reasonable cost, without generating fiscal pressures. In these economies, the public system often provides coverage for a small share of the population, and in some cases, this coverage is insufficient to protect against the risk of illness among those covered.

[24]The health reform, passed by the United States Congress in March 2010, could raise government expenditure by an additional $427 billion over a period of 10 years, according to Congressional Budget Office (CBO) estimates. The spending increases would reflect primarily an expansion in coverage of $938 billion, partially offset by reductions in growth of Medicare payment rates of approximately $330 billion. The reform package also included significant revenue measures that would more than offset the projected increase in spending, generating a net fiscal savings of $143 billion, or about 1 percent of today's GDP (0.1 percent of GDP per year on average).

Table 2.5. Public Health Expenditure in Advanced Economies
(In percent of GDP)

	1960	1970	1980	1990	2000	2007	Change, 1960-2007	Change, 1970-2007
Australia	1.9	3.1	3.9	4.6	5.5	6.0	4.1	2.9
Austria	3.0	3.3	5.1	6.1	7.6	7.7	4.7	4.4
Belgium	...	...	...	6.5	...	...	...	...
Canada	2.3	4.8	5.3	6.6	6.2	7.1	4.8	2.3
Czech Republic	...	...	...	4.6	5.9	5.8	...	...
Denmark	...	6.6	7.9	6.9	6.8	8.2	...	1.6
Finland	2.1	4.1	5.0	6.2	5.1	6.1	4	2.0
France	2.4	4.1	5.6	6.4	8.0	8.7	6.3	4.6
Germany	...	4.4	6.6	6.3	8.2	8.0	...	3.6
Greece	...	2.3	3.3	3.5	4.7	5.8	...	3.5
Hungary	...	...	...	6.3	4.9	5.2	...	...
Iceland	2.0	3.1	5.5	6.8	7.7	7.7	5.7	4.6
Ireland	2.8	4.1	6.8	4.4	4.6	6.1	3.3	2.0
Italy	...	...	...	6.1	5.8	6.7	...	...
Japan	1.8	3.2	4.7	4.6	6.2	6.6	4.8	3.4
Korea	...	...	0.8	1.6	2.1	3.5	...	...
Luxembourg	...	2.8	4.8	5.0	5.2	6.6	...	3.8
Mexico	...	...	...	1.8	2.4	2.7	...	...
Netherlands	...	4.1	5.1	5.4	5.0	7.3	...	1.4
New Zealand	...	4.2	5.2	5.7	6.0	7.1	...	2.9
Norway	2.2	4.0	5.9	6.3	6.9	7.5	5.3	3.5
Poland	...	...	...	4.4	3.9	4.6	...	...
Portugal	...	1.5	3.4	3.8	6.4	7.1	...	5.6
Slovak Republic	...	...	...	...	4.9	5.2	...	...
Spain	0.9	2.3	4.2	5.1	5.2	6.1	5.2	3.8
Sweden	...	5.8	8.2	7.4	7.0	7.4	...	1.6
Switzerland	...	...	...	4.3	5.6	6.4	...	...
Turkey	...	...	0.7	1.6	3.1	4.1	...	...
United Kingdom	3.3	3.9	5.0	4.9	5.6	6.9	3.6	3.0
United States	1.2	2.6	3.7	4.8	5.9	7.3	6.1	4.7
Average (PPP GDP weighted)							5.5	3.9

Sources: OECD Health Database (2009d).
Note: Data for actual or closest year available.

Reforms of the health care systems will need to take into account the different mixes of public and private financing and service provision. For example, the United Kingdom and Italian systems comprise largely public financing and public provision; the Canadian and French systems are characterized by public financing and private provision; and the U.S. system is roughly split between public and private financing and mostly private provision. Across these different systems, both public and private health spending has increased as a percentage of GDP.

Various reforms to contain spending growth and/or improve the efficiency of spending could be considered. Past efforts in this area—including budget caps in a number of European countries in the 1980s, internal market reforms in the United Kingdom in the 1990s, and managed care in the United States in the 1990s—provide valuable lessons for future reforms (Appendix 7), although the appropriate policies will be country-specific, and depend on existing systems. Many of the reforms involve difficult tradeoffs, as they would result in a reduction in the quantity of services financed by the public sector. In light of the tremendous welfare gains produced by health advances (Murphy and Topel, 2006), the principal challenge will be to contain the growth of spending while ensuring broad access to high quality health care.

Supply-side

- *Reimburse providers using case-based payment or global budgets rather than fee-for-service.* This option is important for both advanced and emerging economies. Fee-for-service, which is prevalent in both the United States and in Europe (Belgium, Denmark, France, Germany, and Luxembourg), gives physicians financial incentives to deliver additional services. Case-based payment methods, such as capitation and diagnosis-related groups that bundle different services into one lump sum, are an alternative. There is evidence that moving from fee-for-service to prospective payment can reduce expenditure between 10 and 20 percent (Eggleston and Yip, 2004). On average, switching from fee-for-service to prospective payment methods might reduce spending by 0.1 to 0.2 percent of GDP.[25] To avoid adverse effects on health outcomes, mechanisms should be in place to ensure that providers do not reduce the quality of care or exclude less healthy patients. Greater use of the principles of supply-side control embodied in managed care (such as that

[25]See Appendix 7 for the methodology used to estimate potential expenditure savings from various reforms.

provided by health maintenance organizations) is also an option for controlling costs while maintaining quality care (Cutler, McClellan, and Newhouse, 2000). Another option is to implement and maintain a hard budget constraint through a global cap on provider payments, which by construction will contain spending.[26]

- *Reduce the generosity of the publicly financed benefits package.* This option is more relevant for advanced than emerging economies, as public health services are more generous in the former. These reforms would encourage the financing of some health care by the private sector, which already plays an important—but varying—role in all countries. For example, in Canada, most prescription drugs are not covered by public funds, but rather by private health insurance.
- *Strengthen evaluations of the cost-effectiveness of medical treatments and technology.* In the short term, this is most relevant for advanced economies. Many countries (the United Kingdom, Australia, Netherlands, Sweden, and Finland) have established government bodies that assess the cost-effectiveness of new and existing technologies. Declining to pay for treatments that add small benefits at high incremental costs signals to the R&D sector to develop cost-effective technology. However, such a policy could also reduce the pace of innovation in some areas, which could lower dynamic efficiency (Jena and Philipson, 2007).
- *Implement health information technology (IT) to increase the efficiency of service delivery.* The use of health IT varies widely across advanced economies. This could include, for example, improved data on patient histories (OECD, 2008b). In advanced countries, assuming public health spending is 6½ percent of GDP on average, widespread implementation of health IT could reduce spending by 0.2 percent of GDP.

Demand-side

- *Increase cost-sharing to discourage moral hazard.* This option is more appropriate for advanced economies, where public health expenditure is at relatively high levels. Higher copayments or coinsurance rates for patients would shift some of the costs onto households and could help rationalize the utilization of health care services. A 5 percent increase in the share of cost patients absorb for outpatient care could, on average,

[26]For global caps to be effective, it is important that governments tighten budget constraints for both subnational governments and hospitals (Kornai, 2009; and Crivelli, Leive, and Stratmann, 2010).

reduce spending by 0.1 percent of GDP. The magnitude of any savings will depend on the extent to which other services are complements or substitutes.

- *Reduce tax expenditures for private health insurance.* In countries where private health insurance contributions are exempt from taxation, favorable tax treatment should be reconsidered. The size of these tax expenditures can be large, and some argue this subsidy leads to "overinsurance" (Feldstein, 1973). This issue is most often discussed in the U.S. context—where these benefits amount to about 2 percent of GDP— in light of its employment-based, private insurance system. However, subsidies for private insurance also exist in Australia, Denmark, and Greece.

CHAPTER

3 Tax Reform: Principles, Context, and Administration

Increasing the Tax[27] Ratio: Principles and Experience

For countries looking to substantially increase tax revenue, standard principles (equity, efficiency, ease of implementation) apply—but their application faces emerging challenges:

- *Equity*. Substantially increased inequality in many countries over recent years[28] heightens equity concerns as reflected, for instance, in the increased attention paid to high net wealth individuals (OECD, 2009c). Heavy age-related government spending results in large lifetime transfers towards the baby-boomers, so inter-generational equity suggests they might reasonably bear a substantial part of any increased tax burden (through consumption taxation, for example, which reaches them when they spend accumulated savings);
- *Efficiency*. Uncoordinated tax-setting, given the increased international mobility of capital, goods, and people, can lead to collectively inefficient outcomes. This heightens the case for international cooperation and, in its absence, strengthens the efficiency case for taxing relatively immobile bases (notably real estate and natural resources). Changed understanding of efficient policy—notably in relation to the climate, and perhaps taxation of the financial sector—and the prospect of sluggish growth may also impact the preferred tax mix; and
- *Implementation*. New approaches are required to collect taxes more effectively, including stronger international collaboration, enhanced legal frameworks, strengthened compliance strategies and collection systems, and intensified use of new technologies (to support real-time information

[27] 'Tax' is interpreted throughout as including social contributions.

[28] Documented and discussed in, for instance, Cohen, St. Paul, and Piketty (2008).

management, increased use of pre-populated returns, electronic tax invoices, and, with potential implications for policy design, more extensive personalized pricing).[29]

Theory gives little practical guidance on how best to increase the tax ratio—beyond the unspectacular prescription that if policy is initially optimal, all marginal tax rates be increased equi-proportionally. At an optimum, the welfare cost of changing some tax instrument to raise an additional dollar of revenue—its *marginal cost of public funds (MCPF)*—must be the same for all instruments: otherwise, welfare could be increased without loss of revenue by shifting from the instrument with a higher MCPF to one with a lower one. Starting from such an optimum, the best way to raise additional revenue is by increasing all marginal tax rates in the same proportion.[30] More generally (and plausibly), the first place to look for more revenue is the tax instrument with the lowest MCPF.

There is no consensus on the precise MCPFs of alternative tax instruments, but there is increasing evidence on their relative efficiency. Calculating MCPFs requires taking views on both efficiency (estimates vary widely) and equity (values differ), and so cannot yet firmly guide policy. Empirical work has, though, led to some broad consensus that:

- *The corporate income tax can be particularly distortionary.* Tax effects on investment,[31] and hence long-run growth, can be powerful;[32] and
- *Broad-based consumption taxes and property taxes are less harmful to growth than income taxes.*[33] Taxing consumption is equivalent to taxing accumulated assets and labor income: so it falls partly on a completely inelastic base—previously existing assets—and partly on a base less internationally mobile than capital income.

What contribution could relatively efficient tax policy measures make toward fiscal adjustment in advanced countries with large fiscal gaps? As will be

[29]Cowell (2008) discusses the technical possibilities and inherent limitations.

[30]Strictly, this is true only for small revenue increases.

[31]See for instance the reviews in Hassett and Hubbard (2002) and in relation to foreign direct investment, de Mooij and Ederveen (2003).

[32]Some argue that capital income should not be taxed at all, but the theoretical case is not overwhelming. Auerbach (2006) reviews this debate.

[33]Kneller, Bleaney, and Gemmell (1999) find consumption taxes to be more conducive to growth than direct taxation; Lee and Gordon (2005) find a strong negative impact of the corporate tax on growth. Arnold (2008) finds property taxes to be the most and corporate taxes the least growth-supportive. Myles (2009a, b) reviews the theoretical and empirical literatures.

Table 3.1. Estimated Potential Revenue Increases in Advanced G-20 Countries with Large Adjustment Needs[1]
(In percent of GDP)

Country	Reduce VAT policy GAP by half	Tobacco and alcohol excises [2]	Fuel excises [3 4]	Property taxes [5]	Total	VAT at 10 percent rate [6]	Full auctioning / Taxation of carbon emissions [7]	Total
France	3.8	0.1	0.3	1	5.1	n/a	0.2	5.3
Germany	2.4	0.2	0.3	1	3.8	n/a	0.6	4.5
Italy	3.1	0.3	0.3	1	4.6	n/a	0.5	5.1
Japan	0.3	0.9	0.3	1	2.4	2.6	0	5.0
United Kingdom	3.3	0	0.2	0	3.5	n/a	0.5	5.0
United States	0	0.3	0.6	0	0.9	4.5	0.8	6.1
Unweighted avg.	2.1	0.3	0.3	0.7	3.4	...	0.4	...
Weighted avg. (GDP) [8]	1.1	0.3	0.4	0.4	2.2	...	0.5	...

Sources: Staff estimates and other estimates as discussed in the Tax Policy Options section below.

[1]Figures do not include any increases from base broadening or rate increases in income taxes.

[2]Based upon raising rates for alcohol and tobacco to the 2006 average level of each tax across the six countries shown, where existing rates are below the mean.

[3]Based on raising gasoline and diesel rates by 10 cents per liter in each case other than the United States.

[4]Raising the U.S. tax to 30 cents per liter would raise an additional 0.6 percentage points of GDP existing in the United States.

[5]Increase revenue from property taxes to yield average ratio to GDP in the United States, Canada, and the United Kingdom.

[6]For Japan, estimate of increased revenue from doubling VAT rate to 10 percent; for the United States, approximation of receipts from introduction of broad based federal VAT at 10 percent.

[7]Estimates for European countries derived by weighting allocation of emission rights based upon per country levels of emissions in 2007; a small proportion of these revenues would represent double counting of the carbon emission externality correcting portion of fuel excises.

apparent, it is not possible in such an exercise to go beyond an illustrative approach. That said, however, in the United States, the United Kingdom, France, Germany, Japan, and Italy, for example (Table 3.1), reasonably efficient possible measures for excises, real property taxes, and VAT policy improvements, and the introduction of efficient carbon prices in the United States and Europe (with the revenues captured by government), could raise perhaps a weighted average of 2.8 percent of GDP. If Japan were to increase the rate of its already efficient VAT to 10 percent, and the United States to introduce a broad based VAT at the same rate, an additional 2.6 and 4.5 percent of GDP, respectively, could be raised. And these approximations do not include estimates of any increases in overall income tax revenues.[34]

[34]For these six advanced G-20 countries, top marginal PIT rates are already quite high. Considerably more revenue could be raised, however, by broadening tax bases, and/or by altering the intermediate marginal rate schedules in the personal income tax.

Current Tax Structures[35]

Initial positions—tax levels and the mix of taxes—vary greatly:

- *Tax revenue in percent of GDP* (Table 3.2) varies from under 10 percent to over 40 percent. Tax ratios tend to increase with per capita income, but this is far from a complete explanation of the differences: they vary widely even at similar levels of income (Figure 3.1). Nontax revenues, of course, can make an important contribution to overall revenue effort, especially in resource-rich countries making heavy use of royalties or state enterprises: Saudi Arabia presents an extreme case (see Figure 3.2); and
- *Relative reliance on different revenue sources* also varies greatly (Table 3.3). The empirical literature finds in particular that reliance on income taxes increases with national income (Martinez-Vasquez, Vulovic, and Liu, 2009), and somewhat tentatively, that reliance on labor taxation is lower the higher is the dependency ratio, suggesting an unwillingness of workers to finance the elderly.[36]

These deep differences point to the need for country-specificity in designing revenue adjustment programs. There are nevertheless common themes, from both design and administrative perspectives.

Tax Policy Options

Tax reform must be considered as a package, but in light of common lessons and challenges on key instruments. What matters for the fairness of a tax system, for instance, is not the distributional impact of any tax considered in isolation, but that of all taxes (and indeed spending) combined. While 'tax-by-tax' policy design is thus to be avoided, effective reform does require recognizing the limits and potential of each instrument.[37]

---

[35]Reflecting data availability, the discussion of revenue issues focuses on a slightly different set of countries from that discussed in the expenditure section. Here, we focus on the union of the G-20 (including only EU countries that are direct members) and all other OECD countries.

[36]See Razin and others (2002); Shelton (2008), however, finds no such effect when the dependency ratio is defined solely in terms of the elderly.

[37]Potential tax measures affecting the financial sector are not discussed here, as they were the subject of extensive work simultaneously undertaken for the G-20. Nor, for brevity, are wealth taxes, which, whatever merit may be seen in them, have proved particularly vulnerable to tax planning, erosion, and international tax competition.

Table 3.2. OECD and Other G-20 Countries: Tax Revenue Structure[1]
(In percent of GDP)

	Last Available Year	Total Revenue and Social Security Contributions[3]	Tax Revenue	Taxes on Income, Profits, and Capital Gains: Total	of which: Individual	of which: Corporations and Other Enterprises	of which: Unallocable	Social Security Taxes	Taxes on Payroll and Workforce	Property Taxes	Domestic Taxes on Goods and Services: Total	of which: General sales, turnover or VAT	of which: Excises[2]	of which: Other	International Trade Taxes: Total	Import duties	of which: Export duties	Other
Argentina	2008	33.2	31.1	5.3	1.7	3.3	0.3	5.1	2.3	3.2	9.5	7.8	1.7	0.0	4.4	0.9	3.5	0.0
Australia	2007	37.1	30.8	18.4	11.3	7.1	0.0	0.0	1.4	2.7	7.7	4.0	3.0	0.0	0.5	0.5	0.0	0.0
Austria	2007	48.0	42.3	12.7	7.2	5.0	0.5	14.2	2.7	0.6	11.9	8.0	3.6	0.3	0.0	0.0	0.0	0.0
Belgium	2007	48.1	43.9	16.5	6.2	10.2	0.0	13.6	0.0	2.3	11.0	7.5	3.5	0.0	0.0	0.0	0.0	0.0
Brazil	2008	36.6	35.8	6.7	2.5	2.8	1.4	13.7	0.0	0.6	10.5	9.0	0.2	0.0	0.6	0.6	0.0	0.0
Canada	2007	40.5	33.3	16.6	12.4	3.7	0.5	4.8	0.7	3.3	7.6	4.5	1.7	0.0	0.2	0.2	0.0	0.0
China	2008	20.9	18.0	5.0	1.2	3.7	0.0	...	...	0.3	11.8	8.5	0.9	2.5	-1.4	0.6	-2.0	0.0
Czech Republic	2007	42.0	37.4	9.4	9.1	0.3	0.0	16.2	0.0	0.4	10.4	6.6	3.8	0.0	0.0	0.0	0.0	0.0
Denmark	2007	55.6	48.7	29.0	14.8	14.0	0.3	1.0	0.2	1.9	16.4	10.4	6.0	0.0	0.0	0.0	0.0	0.0
Finland	2007	47.4	43.0	16.9	5.2	11.7	0.0	11.9	0.0	1.1	12.9	8.7	4.2	0.0	0.0	0.0	0.0	0.0
France	2007	49.6	43.7	10.4	7.5	3.0	0.0	16.2	1.2	3.5	10.8	7.4	3.0	0.0	0.0	0.0	0.0	0.0
Germany	2007	43.9	36.2	11.3	9.1	2.2	0.0	13.2	0.0	0.9	10.6	7.0	3.2	0.0	0.0	0.0	0.0	0.0
Greece	2007	40.0	32.0	7.5	4.7	2.6	0.2	11.7	0.0	1.4	11.3	8.3	2.8	0.2	0.0	0.0	0.0	0.0
Hungary	2007	44.8	39.5	10.0	7.1	2.8	0.0	12.9	0.6	0.8	14.5	7.9	4.2	2.4	0.0	0.0	0.0	0.0
Iceland	2007	47.9	40.9	18.5	6.3	10.0	2.2	3.1	0.0	2.5	15.7	11.6	4.2	0.0	0.4	0.4	0.0	0.0
India[3]	2007	22.8	18.6	6.3	2.2	4.1	0.0	...	...	...	2.6	...	2.6	...	2.2	2.2	...	...
Indonesia[4]	2008	20.4	13.3	6.6	...	...	...	...	...	0.5	5.3	4.2	1.0	...	0.7	0.5	0.3	...
Ireland	2007	35.8	30.8	12.1	8.7	3.4	0.0	4.7	0.2	2.5	10.9	7.4	3.5	0.0	0.0	0.0	0.0	0.0
Italy	2007	46.9	43.5	14.7	11.1	3.8	-0.3	13.0	0.0	2.1	11.0	6.2	3.0	0.4	0.0	0.0	0.0	0.0
Japan	2007	31.0	28.3	10.3	5.5	4.8	0.0	10.3	0.0	2.5	4.9	2.5	1.8	0.0	0.2	0.2	0.0	0.0
Korea	2007	25.0	26.5	8.4	4.4	4.0	0.0	5.5	0.1	3.4	7.5	4.2	3.1	0.0	0.8	0.8	0.0	0.0
Luxembourg	2007	41.0	36.5	12.8	7.4	5.4	0.0	10.2	0.0	3.6	9.9	5.9	4.0	0.0	0.0	0.0	0.0	0.0

Table 3.2 *(concluded)*

	Last Available Year	Total Revenue and Social Security Contributions[3]	Tax Revenue	Taxes on Income, Profits, and Capital Gains: Total	of which: Individual	of which: Corporations and Other Enterprises	of which: Unallocable	Social Security Taxes	Taxes on Payroll and Workforce	Property Taxes	Domestic Taxes on Goods and Services: Total	of which: General sales, turnover or VAT	of which: Excises[2]	of which: Other	International Trade Taxes: Total	of which: Import duties	of which: Export duties	of which: Other
Mexico	2007	21.4	18.0	5.0	…	…	5.0	2.8	0.3	0.3	9.2	3.7	0.4	0.0	0.3	0.3	0.0	0.0
Netherlands	2007	45.8	37.5	10.9	7.7	3.3	0.0	13.6	0.0	1.2	11.0	7.5	3.5	0.0	0.0	0.0	0.0	0.0
New Zealand	2007	…	35.7	22.5	15.0	5.1	2.4	0.0	0.0	0.1	10.5	8.4	2.1	0.0	1.0	1.0	0.0	0.0
Norway	2007	56.1	43.6	21.0	4.9	16.1	0.0	9.1	0.0	0.6	11.7	8.3	3.3	0.0	0.1	0.1	0.0	0.0
Poland	2007	40.0	34.9	8.0	3.1	5.0	0.0	12.0	0.0	1.2	13.2	8.3	4.9	0.0	0.0	0.0	0.0	0.0
Portugal	2007	43.1	36.4	9.4	5.6	3.9	0.0	11.7	0.0	1.4	13.6	8.1	5.4	0.0	0.0	0.0	0.0	0.0
Russia	2007	40.0	35.9	10.0	4.0	6.0	0.0	5.1	…	…	6.0	5.1	0.8	0.0	8.6	1.5	7.1	0.0
Saudi Arabia	2008	67.3	6.7	0.5	…	0.5	0.0	…	…	…	…	…	…	…	0.8	0.8	…	…
Slovak Republic	2007	34.7	29.4	5.8	0.2	5.3	0.3	11.7	0.0	0.4	11.3	7.5	3.8	0.0	0.0	0.0	0.0	0.0
South Africa	2007	…	30.9	16.6	8.5	8.2	0.0	0.6	0.3	1.7	10.4	7.5	2.5	0.0	1.3	1.3	0.0	0.0
Spain	2007	41.0	37.2	12.3	4.6	7.4	0.3	12.1	0.0	3.0	9.5	6.3	3.2	0.0	0.0	0.0	0.0	0.0
Sweden	2007	53.6	48.3	18.7	14.9	3.8	0.0	12.6	2.7	1.2	12.9	9.2	3.6	0.1	0.0	0.0	0.0	0.0
Switzerland	2007	36.8	28.9	13.2	2.3	11.0	0.0	6.7	0.0	2.4	6.4	3.9	2.5	0.0	0.2	0.2	0.0	0.0
Turkey	2007	31.7	23.7	5.6	4.0	1.6	0.0	5.1	0.0	0.9	11.0	5.1	5.5	0.0	0.3	0.3	0.0	0.0
United Kingdom	2007	37.8	36.1	14.3	10.9	3.4	0.0	6.6	0.0	4.5	10.5	6.6	3.4	0.0	0.0	0.0	0.0	0.0
United States	2007	29.9	28.3	13.9	10.8	3.1	0.0	6.6	0.0	3.1	4.5	2.2	1.1	0.0	0.2	0.2	0.0	0.0
Unweighted average[5]			33.3	11.9	6.9	5.3	0.4	8.8	0.4	1.8	10.2	6.8	3.0	0.2	0.6	0.3	0.2	0.0

Sources: IMF, Government Finance Statistics; International Financial Statistics; World Economic Outlook; and OECD.

[1]General government.

[2]Including taxes on specific services.

[3]Gross tax revenue of the central government plus state tax revenue.

[4]Central government.

[5]For each revenue item, only countries for which data are available are included in the calculation.

Figure 3.1. OECD and Other G-20 Countries: Tax Revenue and GDP Per Capita

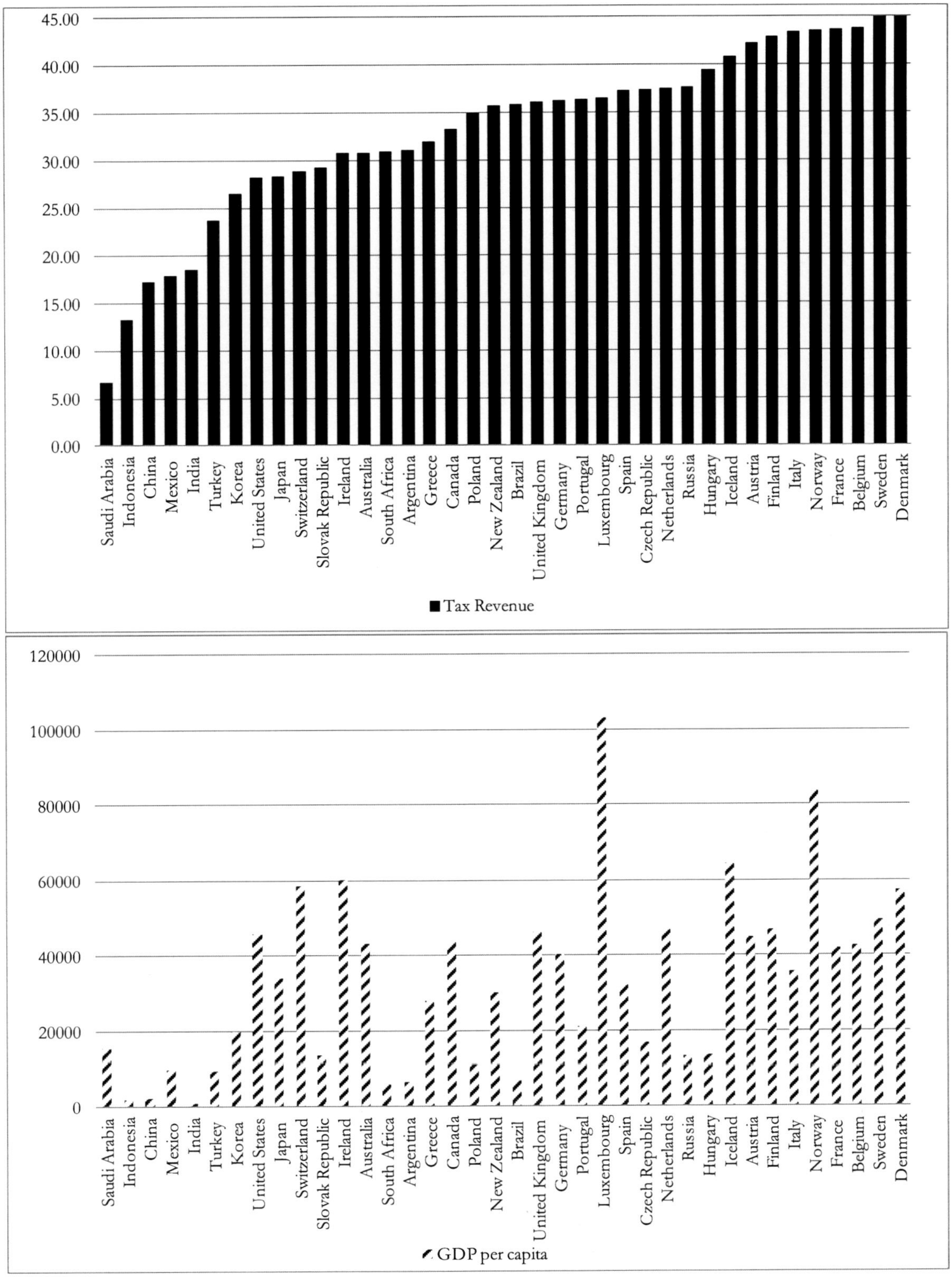

Sources: IMF; and OECD.

Figure 3.2. OECD and Other G-20 Countries: Tax Revenue Structure
(In percent of total tax revenue)

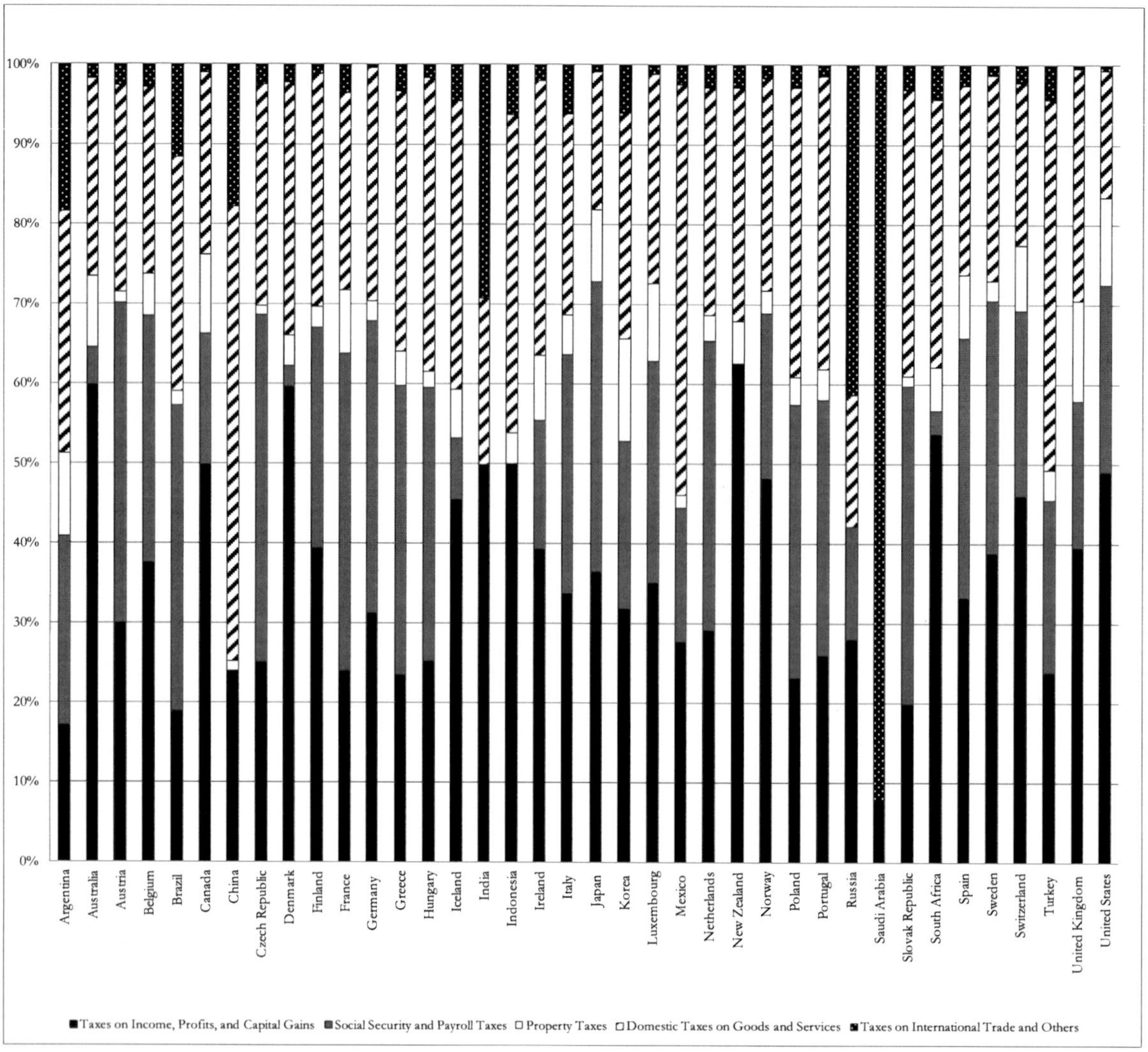

Sources: IMF; and OECD.

Table 3.3. Tax Revenue Structure[1]
(In percent of tax revenues)

	Last Available Year	Tax Revenue	Taxes on Income, Profits, and Capital Gains: Total	of which: Individual	of which: Corporations and Other Enterprises	of which: Unallocable	Social Security Taxes	Taxes on Payroll and Workforce	Property Taxes	Domestic Taxes on Goods and Services: Total	of which: General sales, turnover or VAT	of which: Excises[2]	of which: Other	International Trade Taxes: Total	of which: Import duties	of which: Export duties	of which: Other
Argentina	2008	100	17.1	5.5	10.6	1.0	16.4	7.3	10.4	30.4	25.0	5.4	0.1	14.1	2.8	11.3	0.1
Australia	2007	100	59.8	36.7	23.1	0.0	0.0	4.7	8.9	24.9	13.0	9.6	0.0	1.7	1.7	0.0	0.0
Austria	2007	100	30.0	22.5	5.8	1.7	33.7	6.3	1.4	26.0	18.3	7.6	0.0	0.0	0.0	0.0	0.0
Belgium	2007	100	37.5	29.3	8.2	0.1	31.0	0.0	5.1	23.5	16.3	7.2	0.0	0.0	0.0	0.0	0.0
Brazil	2008	100	18.8	7.1	7.9	3.8	38.4	0.0	1.8	29.4	25.0	0.6	0.0	1.6	1.6	0.0	0.0
Canada	2007	100	49.8	37.4	11.0	1.4	14.4	2.0	9.9	22.9	13.6	5.2	0.0	0.7	0.7	0.0	0.0
China	2008	100	27.5	6.9	20.6	0.0	...	...	1.5	65.6	47.3	4.7	13.6	-7.6	3.3	-10.8	0.0
Czech Republic	2007	100	25.1	11.6	13.4	0.0	43.5	0.0	1.2	27.7	17.6	10.1	0.0	0.0	0.0	0.0	0.0
Denmark	2007	100	59.6	51.7	7.4	0.5	2.0	0.5	3.8	31.8	21.4	10.4	0.0	0.0	0.0	0.0	0.0
Finland	2007	100	39.3	30.3	9.0	0.0	27.7	0.0	2.6	29.3	19.5	9.8	0.0	0.0	0.0	0.0	0.0
France	2007	100	23.9	17.1	6.8	0.0	37.1	2.8	8.0	24.6	17.0	7.0	0.0	0.0	0.0	0.0	0.0
Germany	2007	100	31.2	25.1	6.1	0.0	36.6	0.0	2.5	29.2	19.4	8.7	0.0	0.1	0.1	0.0	0.0
Greece	2007	100	23.4	14.7	8.0	0.6	36.4	0.0	4.3	32.5	22.8	9.2	0.6	0.1	0.1	0.0	0.0
Hungary	2007	100	25.2	18.2	7.0	0.0	32.7	1.5	2.0	36.9	20.0	10.9	6.0	0.1	0.1	0.0	0.0
Iceland	2007	100	45.4	33.9	6.1	5.4	7.7	0.1	6.1	36.1	25.9	10.2	0.0	1.0	1.0	0.0	0.0
India[3]	2007	100	33.7	11.7	22.0	0.0	...	...	...	14.1	...	14.1	...	11.9	11.9	...	...
Indonesia[4]	2008	100	49.7	...	...	...	...	...	3.8	39.6	31.8	7.8	...	5.5	3.5	2.1	...
Ireland	2007	100	39.3	28.4	10.9	0.0	15.4	0.7	8.2	34.4	24.1	10.3	0.0	0.0	0.0	0.0	0.0
Italy	2007	100	33.7	25.6	8.8	-0.7	30.0	0.0	4.9	25.2	14.2	7.0	0.9	0.0	0.0	0.0	0.0
Japan	2007	100	36.4	19.6	16.8	0.0	36.4	0.0	9.0	17.3	8.8	6.5	0.0	0.6	0.6	0.0	0.0
Korea	2007	100	31.8	16.7	15.1	0.0	20.8	0.2	12.8	28.3	15.8	11.5	0.0	3.0	3.0	0.0	0.0
Luxembourg	2007	100	35.0	20.1	14.9	0.0	27.8	0.0	9.8	26.3	15.3	10.9	0.0	0.0	0.0	0.0	0.0

Table 3.3 *(concluded)*

	Last Available Year	Tax Revenue	Taxes on Income, Profits, and Capital Gains: Total	of which: Individual	of which: Corporations and Other Enterprises	of which: Unallocable	Social Security Taxes	Taxes on Payroll and Workforce	Property Taxes	Domestic Taxes on Goods and Services: Total	of which: General sales, turnover or VAT	of which: Excises [2]	of which: Other	International Trade Taxes: Total	of which: Import duties	of which: Export duties	of which: Other
Mexico	2007	100	27.7	...	...	27.7	15.3	1.4	1.7	51.4	20.4	2.5	0.0	1.7	1.7	0.0	0.0
Netherlands	2007	100	29.1	20.4	8.7	0.0	36.2	0.0	3.3	28.5	19.8	8.7	0.0	0.0	0.0	0.0	0.0
New Zealand	2007	100	62.9	42.1	14.2	6.7	0.0	0.0	5.3	29.4	23.5	5.9	0.0	2.9	2.9	0.0	0.0
Norway	2007	100	48.1	22.1	26.0	0.0	20.8	0.0	2.8	26.7	19.1	7.7	0.0	0.2	0.2	0.0	0.0
Poland	2007	100	23.1	15.2	7.9	0.0	34.3	0.0	3.4	36.2	23.5	12.7	0.0	0.1	0.1	0.0	0.0
Portugal	2007	100	25.9	15.8	10.1	0.0	32.1	0.0	3.8	36.8	24.1	12.7	0.0	0.0	0.0	0.0	0.0
Russia	2007	100	27.9	11.1	16.8	0.0	14.1	...	...	16.6	14.2	2.3	0.0	23.9	4.2	19.8	0.0
Saudi Arabia	2008	100	7.6	...	7.6	0.0	...	...	...	...	...	...	...	12.5	12.5	...	...
Slovak Republic	2007	100	19.9	8.6	10.2	1.0	39.8	0.0	1.4	35.8	22.9	12.9	0.0	0.0	0.0	0.0	0.0
South Africa	2007	100	53.7	27.3	26.3	0.0	1.9	1.0	5.4	33.6	24.3	8.2	0.1	4.3	4.2	0.0	0.1
Spain	2007	100	33.1	19.8	12.4	0.9	32.6	0.0	8.0	23.7	16.2	7.5	0.0	0.0	0.0	0.0	0.0
Sweden	2007	100	38.7	30.9	7.9	0.0	26.1	5.7	2.4	25.7	19.1	6.4	0.2	0.0	0.0	0.0	0.0
Switzerland	2007	100	45.9	35.3	10.6	0.0	23.3	0.0	8.2	20.4	13.1	7.3	0.0	0.7	0.7	0.0	0.0
Turkey	2007	100	23.7	17.0	6.8	0.0	21.7	0.0	3.8	46.4	21.3	23.0	0.0	1.2	1.2	0.0	0.0
United Kingdom	2007	100	39.5	30.1	9.4	0.0	18.4	0.0	12.6	29.1	18.2	9.3	0.0	0.1	0.1	0.0	0.0
United States	2007	100	49.0	38.1	11.0	0.0	23.4	0.0	11.0	15.8	7.7	3.9	0.0	0.7	0.7	0.0	0.0
Unweighted average [5]		100	35.0	23.0	11.8	1.4	24.3	1.0	5.5	30.1	20.0	8.5	0.6	2.1	1.6	0.6	0.0

Sources: IMF, Government Finance Statistics; International Finance Statistics; and *World Economic Outlook*.

[1]General government.

[2]Including taxes on specific services.

[3]Gross tax revenue of the central government plus state tax revenue.

[4]Central government.

[5]For each revenue item, only countries for which data are available are included in the calculation.

Table 3.4. Current VAT Rates and Efficiency in G-20 Countries

	C-efficiency	VAT revenues as percent of GDP	Current Standard Rate	Current Other Positive Rates
Canada	50	3.1	5.0	
Japan	69	2.6	5.0	
Australia	51	3.8	10.0	
Indonesia	52	3.7	10.0	5; 10; 15.0
Korea	61	4.2	10.0	
South Africa	65	7.4	14.0	
Mexico	33	3.7	15.0	10.0
United Kingdom	43	6.5	17.5	5.0
China,P.R.: Mainland	68	6.0	17.0	13.0
Russia	48	5.6	18.0	10.0
Turkey	37	5.5	18.0	1.0; 8.0; 26; 40
Germany	50	6.2	19.0	7.0
France	45	7.1	19.6	2.1; 5.5
Italy	39	6.1	20.0	4.0;10.0
Brazil	51	7.3	20.5	Multiple (25 rates)
Argentina	46	6.9	21.0	10.5; 27.0

Sources: IMF staff calculations; International Bureau of Fiscal Documentation (IBFD); and PricewaterhouseCoopers.

Consumption taxes

Value-added tax (VAT)

The VAT is a mainstay of the tax systems of almost all G-20 and emerging countries. Saudi Arabia and the United States are the only G-20 members without one; India is currently introducing a federal level VAT to be coordinated with its relatively new state-level VATs. Elsewhere in the G-20, the VAT raises, on average, over 5 percent of GDP and about 20 percent of revenue (Table 3.4): it has proved a relatively efficient source of revenue[38]—one, that is, with a relatively low MCPF.

However, exemptions and excessive rate differentiation compromise the effectiveness and implementation of the VAT. Exemption—charging no VAT on sales but denying refund of tax paid on inputs—undermines the

[38]Keen and Lockwood (2009b) provide empirical evidence; Ebrill and others (2001); and Bird and Gendron (2007) discuss why; Keen (2009a) reviews evidence on the performance of and current controversies in the VAT.

logic of the VAT by taxing intermediate transactions. Multiple rates are less damaging in policy terms, but the most common rationale—improving equity—is generally unpersuasive for G-20 countries: the rich generally spend *absolutely* more on items which are taxed at low rates to assist the poor; and most G-20 countries have, or could develop, instruments that are better targeted to equity objectives. In the United Kingdom, for example, eliminating zero- and reduced-rating, while increasing income-related benefits to protect the poor, would raise net revenue of around 0.75 percent of GDP (Crawford, Keen and Smith, 2008).[39] Tax administration—and the compliance burden—is also adversely affected by multiple rates and exemptions.

There is substantial scope for improving the revenue performance of the VAT in almost all countries. The effectiveness of a VAT is conveniently assessed by its 'C-efficiency,' defined as VAT revenue divided by the product of the standard rate and aggregate private consumption: for a VAT with no exemptions, a single rate, and full compliance, C-efficiency would be 100 percent.[40] In practice, many VATs are far from this: many countries could raise significant revenue by modestly increasing C-efficiency, with no need to increase the standard rate: Italy, for example, would gain around 2.5 percent of GDP by raising C-efficiency to the G-20 average (Appendix 9).

Broadly speaking, the scope for administrative improvement is especially large in emerging countries, and that for policy improvement, especially large in advanced countries. While informative, C-efficiency measures in themselves give little clue as to precisely where improvements in the VAT might be found. It can, however, be decomposed into components relating to the VAT "compliance gap" and the "policy gap."[41] Table 3.5 illustrates this for selected countries. What is striking is that (though there are, of

[39]The downside is that the withdrawal of these increased benefits may imply higher marginal effective rates of tax over some range of income: an increased distortion to be weighed against the strengthening of the fiscal position.

[40]The nature and limitations of the concept are discussed in Ebrill and others (2001) and OECD (2008b). It is worth noting that there are poor policy structures that can actually increase C-efficiency, under this definition—for example, failure to provide for refunds of excess input credits, exemption of certain intermediate inputs.

[41]The VAT "compliance gap" is defined here as the difference between current VAT collections, and those that would be obtained if the existing VAT law were perfectly enforced; the "policy gap" is defined as the difference between collections under current law, and those that would be obtained if all exemptions not consistent with best practice and all reduced rates were eliminated, in both cases assuming full compliance with the law.

Table 3.5. Additional VAT Revenue from Policy and Administrative Improvements, 2006 Figures

	VAT Revenue in percent of: Tax Revenues	VAT Revenue in percent of: GDP	VAT Rate	C-efficiency	VAT Compliance Gap	VAT Policy Gap	Potential Extra Revenue (in percent of GDP) from:[1] Improved policy: Max. improvement	Improved policy: Reducing gap by half	Improved compliance[2]: Max. compliance	Improved compliance[2]: Reducing gap to 15%
Emerging Economies										
Argentina	29.9	6.9	21.0	46	21	41	4.9	2.3	1.9	0.5
Mexico	20.4	3.7	15.0	33	18	60	5.6	2.8	0.8	0.1
Hungary	30.5	7.4	20.0	49	23	37	4.3	2.2	2.2	0.8
Latvia	39.1	8.3	21.0	49	22	38	5.1	2.5	2.3	0.7
Lithuania	36.1	7.5	18.0	50	22	36	4.3	2.1	2.1	0.7
Brazil	30.7	7.3	17.5	52	n/a	...	3.8	1.9	2.0	0.6
Indonesia	30.1	3.7	10.0	52	n/a	...	1.9	1.0	1.0	0.3
India	17.1	3.0	12.5	35	n/a	...	3.6	1.8	0.8	0.2
China	36.7	6.0	17.0	68	n/a	...	1.0	0.5	1.6	0.5
S. Africa	28.2	7.4	14.0	65	n/a	...	1.6	0.8	2.0	0.6
Bulgaria	39.5	11.8	20.0	68	n/a	...	1.9	1.0	3.2	0.9
Romania	28.6	8.1	19.0	50	n/a	...	4.8	2.4	2.2	0.6
Russia	15.0	5.6	18.0	48	n/a	...	3.7	1.8	1.5	0.4
Turkey	29.3	5.5	18.0	37	n/a	...	6.3	3.2	1.5	0.4
Average	29.1	7.1	18.6	50	21	43	3.8	1.9	1.8	0.5
Advanced Economies							Max. Improvement	Reducing gap by half	Max. compliance	Reducing gap to 7%
France	42.2	7.1	19.6	45	7	52	7.5	3.8	0.5	0.0
Germany	27.1	6.2	16.0	50	10	44	4.9	2.4	0.7	0.2
Italy	21.0	6.1	20.0	39	22	50	6.2	3.1	1.7	1.2
UK	21.7	6.5	17.5	43	13	50	6.5	3.3	1.0	0.5
Australia	12.9	3.8	10.0	51	n/a	...	2.6	1.3	0.6	0.1
Japan	14.2	2.6	5.0	69	n/a	...	0.7	0.3	0.4	0.1
Korea	20.9	4.2	10.0	61	n/a	...	1.8	0.9	0.6	0.1
Canada	9.2	3.1	5.0	50	n/a	...	1.4	0.7	0.3	0.1
Average	21.1	4.9	12.9	51	13	49	3.9	2.0	0.7	0.3

Sources: WEO; GFS; Reckon LLP (2009); and IMF staff estimates.

[1]For countries where no VAT gap estimate is available, the average (21 percent for emerging and 13 percent advanced economies) of those available has been used.

[2]Improving VAT compliance is likely to have an indirect positive effect on income tax compliance which is not reflected in these figures.

course, marked exceptions) while C-efficiencies are much the same for both groups, this reflects the offsetting effects of a significantly higher compliance rate in advanced countries combined with policy design that is, if anything, poorer. For example, the proportional revenue gain from moving to the high level of compliance in France is nearly three times as large for emerging economies as for advanced economies; while that from moving closer to Latvia's efficient policy design is slightly larger in advanced countries than in emerging countries.

Guiding principles for VAT reform include:

- *Reducing exemptions and eliminating reduced rates is generally the best way to increase VAT revenue, unless low efficiency is caused by weak administration.* Much could be done without increasing the standard rate in many countries. In Mexico, for instance, the reduced border rate of 10 percent serves little useful purpose; and the reduced rate in Germany costs 0.8 percent of GDP; on average, even reducing this exemption/rate "policy gap" by half could raise nearly 2 percent of GDP for both emerging and advanced economies.
- *There can be substantial revenue gain from cutting large VAT compliance gaps.* Latvia, for instance, could raise 1.6 percent of GDP by reducing its VAT compliance gap to that of France; reducing the compliance gap to 15 percent in emerging, and 7 percent in advanced, economies could raise an estimated 0.5 percent and 0.3 percent of GDP, respectively.
- *Where neither structure nor administration is problematic, rates could be raised with minimal distortion.* In Japan, for example, C-efficiency is high but the (single) rate is low: substantially increasing the rate in such cases is a reasonably sure way to raise more revenue at minimal welfare cost.

For countries without a VAT, introduction is the leading option for substantially enhancing revenues. In the United States, for example, a VAT at 13 percent might raise 6 percent of GDP (Graetz, 2005; other recent estimates give comparable revenue per percentage point of the VAT rate for a broad-based VAT with few exemptions). Late adopters would benefit from avoiding the errors of 'old' VATs, such as the overly-broad exemptions to which the EU is locked in (Cnossen, 2003).

Excises

Many countries have scope to increase significantly revenues from tobacco and alcohol excises. Receipts are noticeably lower in the emerging G-20

Table 3.6. Excise Revenue from Tobacco and Alcohol Consumption in Selected G-20 Countries
(In percent of GDP)

	Tobacco		Alcohol		Total [1]	
	1995 [2]	2007	1995 [3]	2007	1995	2007
Australia	0.26	0.52	0.14	0.17	0.40	0.69
Brazil	0.35	0.11	0.20	0.10	0.55	0.21
Canada	0.47	0.46	0.13	0.09	0.60	0.55
China [4]	n/a	0.02	n/a	n/a	n/a	n/a
France	0.53	0.52	0.23	0.05	0.76	0.57
Germany	0.57	0.58	0.21	0.14	0.78	0.72
India	0.31	0.23	n/a	n/a	n/a	n/a
Italy	0.53	0.66	0.06	0.07	0.59	0.73
Japan	0.42	0.44	0.42	0.29	0.84	0.73
Korea R.	0.52	0.28	0.54	0.29	1.06	0.58
Mexico	0.14	0.18	0.12	0.19	0.26	0.37
Russia	0.10	0.15	0.40	0.20	0.50	0.35
UK	1.00	0.58	0.75	0.58	1.75	1.15
USA	0.18	0.17	0.15	0.10	0.33	0.27

Sources: IMF; OECD; and national authorities.

[1]Data for Turkey are for combined tobacco and alcohol only, and for 2006 to 2009.

[2]1999 for Australia, 1997 for India, 2000 for Mexico, and 2001 for Russia.

[3]1999 for Australia, 2000 for Mexico, and 1998 for Russia.

[4]Does not include profits from tobacco monopoly.

(Table 3.6), where the arguments for cigarette taxation, in particular, may be especially strong. In the advanced economies, their yield (especially for alcohol) is in trend decline (falling by about 0.5 percentage point of GDP in the United Kingdom since 1995, for instance) reflecting not just changing consumption patterns but also falling real tax rates. Policymakers have moderated rate increases for fear of excessive cross-border shopping and smuggling:[42] enhanced cross-border cooperation, in both design and implementation, may be required to realize the potential gains. The minimum excise rates within the EU illustrate the possibilities, but also the difficulty: politics has meant that many rates are low (zero, for some alcoholic drinks).

[42]Empirical evidence for this is in Lockwood and Migali (2008).

Figure 3.3a. Motor Fuel Tax Revenues
(In percent of GDP)

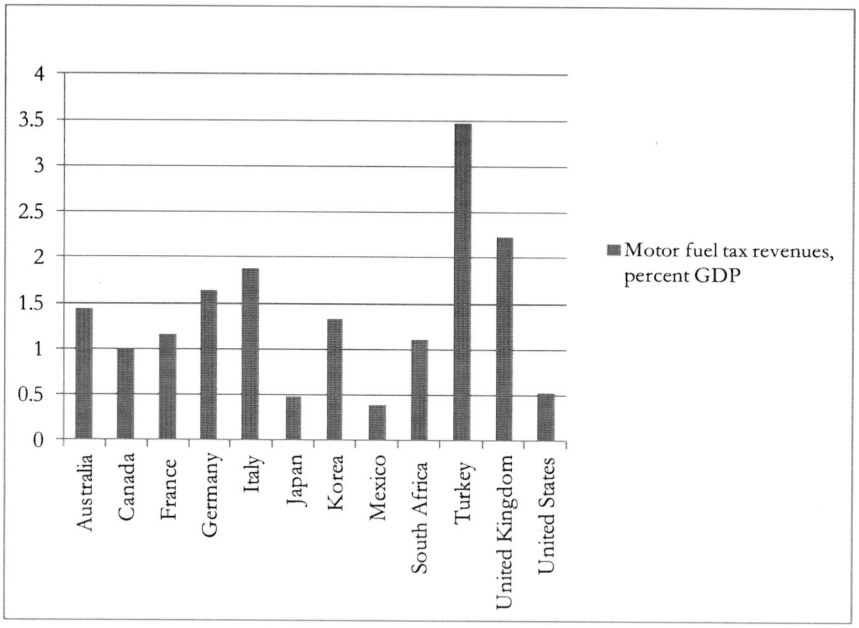

Sources: OECD Revenue Statistics 2009; OECD database of environmental taxes; http://www.taxpolicycenter.org/taxfacts/listdocs.cfm?topic2id=80 Figures for 2007, except Australia (2008); and France, Mexico, Turkey (2006).

Figure 3.3b. Motor Fuel Taxes for Selected G-20 Countries

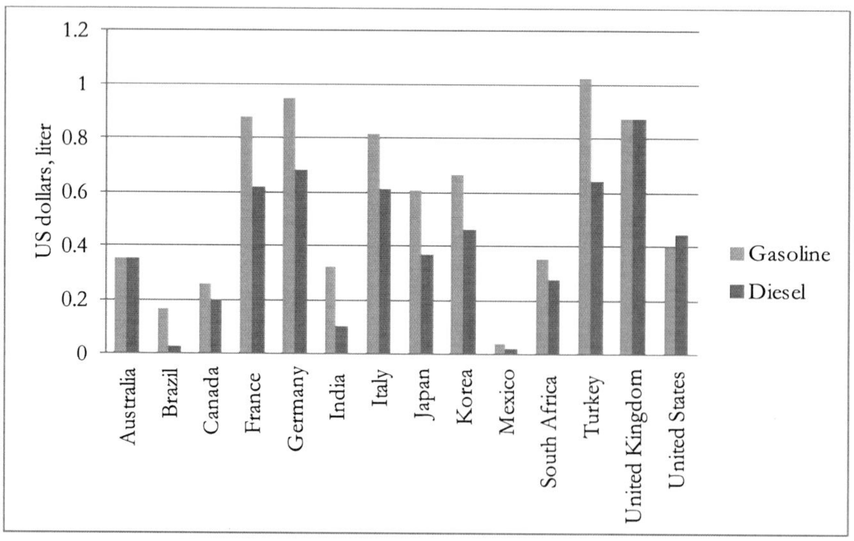

Sources: IEA Prices and Energy Taxes 2009 Third Quarter; Energy Information Administration; Parry and Strand (2010). National taxes and average local taxes combined where appropriate. Figures for 2009 except India (2008); and standard unleaded gasoline, except France, South Africa, Turkey, and the United Kingdom (premium).

The low level of fuel taxation in many advanced countries means that the potential revenue gains from more efficient tax levels are substantial. Among G-20 countries, fuel tax revenues in Japan, Mexico, and the United States are especially low (Figure 3.3a, 3.3b). Coady, and others (2010) project that the forgone revenues in G-20 countries from taxing below $0.30 cents per liter (the lower end of their benchmarks for efficient fuel tax levels) could reach $490 billion by the end of 2010. Possible efficiency gains from the taxation of diesel may be especially marked, given the preferential tax treatment it receives in many G-20 countries (Figure 3.3b). In addition, the fact that fuel taxes are often used as a second-best alternative to more efficient tax instruments (e.g., congestion charges) suggests that the net revenue effect of replacing these components of the fuel tax with their more efficient alternative may be positive.[43]

Car taxes in some cases have unexploited potential. They vary greatly—one-off registration fees, annual ownership fees, taxes on new sales—and some of the concerns to which they are tailored (road use and emissions) are better targeted by other instruments. Nevertheless, this is another convenient tax handle that some could exploit further: Mexico, France, and the United States, for example, raise less than half of the 0.4 percent or so of GDP collected in Germany, Italy, and the United Kingdom. Further, they can be an instrument of progressivity, especially for developing/emerging countries, if rates are varied according to size or type of vehicle.

Scope for new types of excises is limited. The empirical evidence required to warrant rate differentiation across countries is rarely firm enough to outweigh implementation costs, and taxes addressed to environmental harm (beyond fuel excises/carbon taxation) have little revenue potential—that not being their main purpose. Taxing telecom services is sometimes suggested, partly to tap rents that cannot be reached directly. But the drawbacks are substantial: network externalities are important in early stages of the product cycle; distinguishing personal from business use is hard; and auctions can be a more effective way of extracting rents.

[43]These tax increases are only in relatively small part aimed at properly pricing carbon emissions. One study that suggests a tax level of $0.25 per liter includes only, for example, 1.6 cents as the cost of carbon emission (Parry and Small, 2005).

Figure 3.4a. Corporate Income Tax Revenue and CIT Statutory Rate in OECD Countries

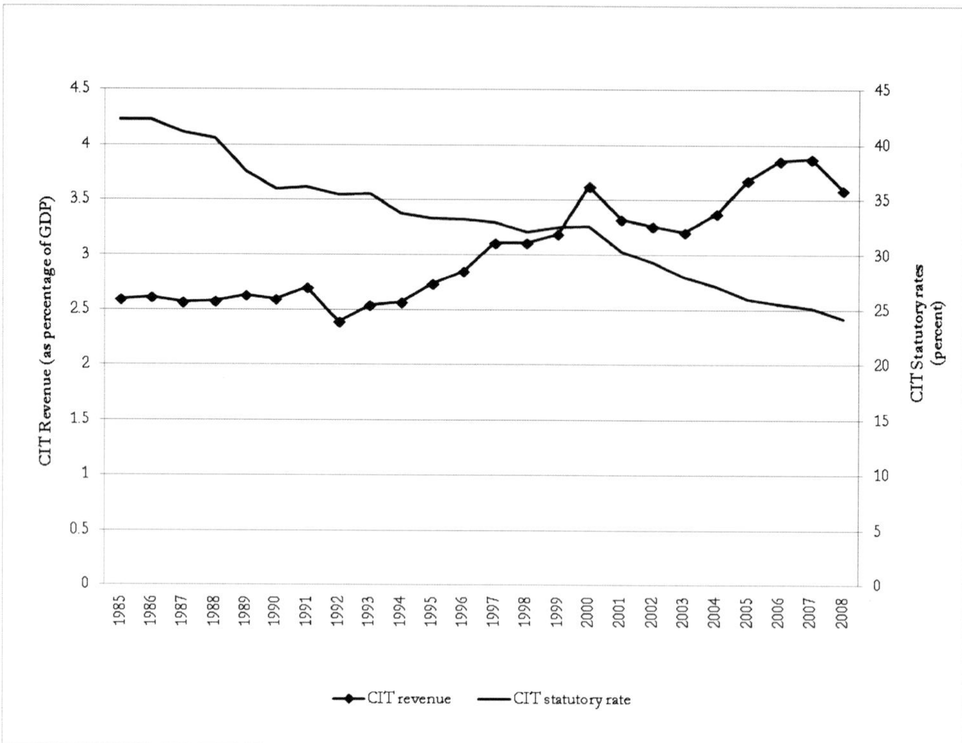

Source: OECD.

Income tax

Corporate income tax (CIT)

The increased international tax competition over the past two decades is likely to continue. There is substantial evidence that the significant decrease in statutory rates of CIT since the mid-1980s (Figure 3.4a)—by an average of about 15 percentage points across the OECD—reflects strategic competition in tax-setting, not simply some common trend (Devereux, Lockwood, and Redoana, 2008). One instance of this is that the highest corporate tax rates in the G-20 (and hence perhaps the greatest pressures for reduction) are found in large economies: notably the United States.[44] Movements towards territorial rather than worldwide taxation in the United Kingdom—that is, taxing corporations only on their income derived within the country, rather than on all of their income no matter where derived if they are headquartered

[44]Most models of tax competition predict that larger countries will set higher tax rates, since for them the revenue gain from cutting tax rates to attract tax base from abroad is smaller relative to the revenue lost from the domestic base (Wilson, 1999).

Figure 3.4b. Corporate Income Tax Rate and CIT Revenue in Selected G-20 Countries, 1995–2008

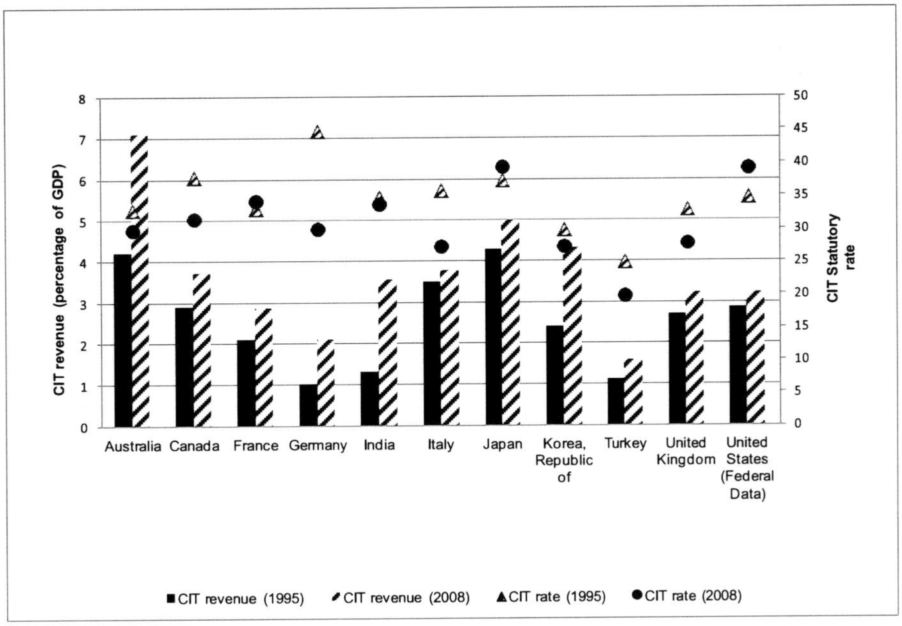

Sources: Government Finance Statistics; International Financial Statistics; *World Economic Outlook*; OECD; and IMF staff estimates.

or otherwise deemed to be domestic companies—as is often also discussed for the United States,[45] are a further symptom of this competitive trend, and would also be a possible source of its intensification.[46]

CIT revenue had, until the crisis, remained strong[47]—but this cannot be relied on looking forward (Figure 3.4b). To the extent that it reflected increased incorporation as CIT rates fell relative to personal income tax rates (PIT) (de Mooij and Nicodeme, 2008), resilience could continue if CIT rates keep falling (though with some offsetting reduction in PIT receipts). Some argue that the strength of CIT revenue reflected rates being above revenue-maximizing levels, but this remains contentious (Brill and Hassett, 2007; and Clausing, 2007) and any such effect must ultimately vanish. The strength of

[45]By the President's Advisory Panel on Federal Tax Reform (2006), for example.

[46]Under worldwide, or "residence-based" taxation, capital importing countries have an incentive to set their tax rate at least as high as that in the capital exporting countries (since doing otherwise simply creates an offsetting liability for the investor when profits are repatriated); under territorial taxation, this incentive disappears; Mullins (2006) elaborates.

[47]Devereux, Griffith, and Klemm (2002).

CIT revenue also reflected a large contribution from the financial sector[48] that has now fallen substantially, and may be permanently reduced by regulatory reform. While there remains scope for base-broadening in many countries, potential revenue gains from this in the G-20 seem fairly modest: there have already been significant base-broadening measures, notably in relation to depreciation (Devereux, Griffiths, and Klemm, 2002) and, in some cases—as with China, and for example, in the EU state aid rules—a scaling-back of incentives.

Unprecedented international coordination would be required to limit/reverse pressures on CIT rates and revenues. Those who see the CIT as particularly damaging to growth would of course welcome its demise. It does though serve as a backstop to the PIT and, potentially, a relatively efficient tax on rents (that is, earnings in excess of a "normal" return to capital). However, given the ease with which profits can be shifted to low-tax jurisdictions, it can play this role fully only if policies are coordinated across countries: the MCPF of the CIT may be much lower when policy is coordinated than from a unilateral perspective. Coordination might take a variety of forms—agreement on minimum tax rates, on scaling back incentives, some form of formulary apportionment, or more limited agreements (to deal with hybrid entities, for instance; see Thuronyi, 2010). The recent progress on combating the use of tax havens, discussed below, is limited to information exchange, and does not address these more sensitive topics of tax rates and design.

Prospects are brighter in resource-rich economies. Though not immune to pressures of international tax competition, the element of location-specific rent in resource returns provides a potentially robust source of relatively non-distorting revenues.[49] This is indeed an important source of revenue in many advanced and emerging countries (Figure 3.5): eleven of the G-20 are major oil and gas producers;[50] others are major ore and metal exporters. Most are sufficiently able to diversify the risks of natural resource exploitation to make profit/cash-flow based instruments more efficient than fixed fees and

[48]Commonly accounting for a fifth or so of CIT revenue pre-crisis: see IMF (2010d) on experience in the United Kingdom.

[49]Over-taxation of rents subsequent to discovery risks deterring exploration, however. The implications of this, and the distinct issues of tax coordination that arise in relation to resources, are discussed in Boadway and Keen (2010).

[50]Argentina, Australia, Brazil, Canada, China, Indonesia, Mexico, Russia, Saudi Arabia, the United Kingdom, and the United States.

Figure 3.5. Minerals Contribution to Total Government Revenues
(In percent of GDP1)

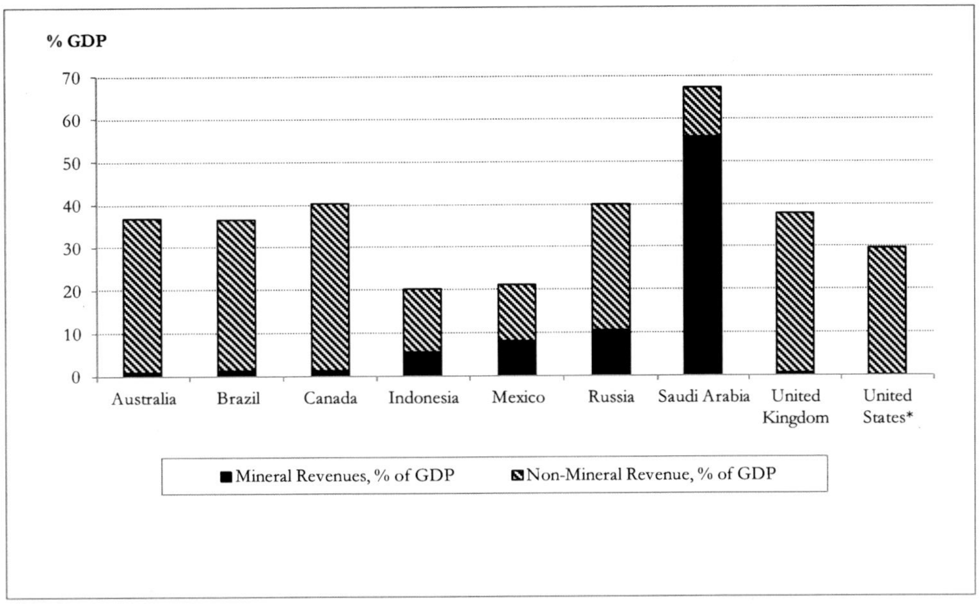

Sources: National authorities; World Economic Outlook; and IMF staff estimates.

Notes: *U.S. mineral revenue data excludes corporate incomes taxes; data for Brazil, Indonesia, and Saudi Arabia reflects 2008 levels; all the rest reflects 2007.

[1]2008 GDP or most recent available year.

royalties, yet some—including the United States and Russia—still place heavy reliance on the latter.[51] Movement towards explicit rent taxation, including through auction, could produce a marked revenue enhancement.[52] This is not to argue that average effective tax rates are necessarily low (in any case, these will vary with price and project), but that tax structures could be modified both to promote investment and to secure for governments higher shares of resource rent in profitable projects.

Personal income tax (PIT)

The personal income tax is generally considered key to the pursuit of equity in the tax system, though the effectiveness of this is tempered by the incentive effects (on both real activity and compliance) of increasing effective

[51]The case for revision of the fiscal terms for oil and gas in Russia has recently been analyzed in Goldsworthy and Zakharova (2010).

[52]The argument for this is developed in Land (2010) and Daniel and others (2010).

Table 3.7. Total Tax Revenue and PIT Revenue as Percent of GDP, and PIT Top Marginal Rates for G-20 Countries[1]

Country	Last Available Year	Total Tax Revenue	PIT Revenue	Ratio PIT to Total Revenue	PIT Top Marginal Rate
Argentina	2008	31.1	1.7	5.5	35
Australia	2007	30.8	11.3	36.7	45
Brazil	2008	35.8	3.2 [2]	8.9	28
Canada	2007	33.3	12.4	37.4	39 / 48.3 [3]
China, P.R.: Mainland	2008	18.0	1.2	6.9	45
France	2007	43.7	7.5	17.1	40
Germany	2007	36.2	9.1	25.1	45
India	2007	18.6	2.2	11.7	30
Indonesia	2008	13.3 [4]	...	...	35
Italy	2007	43.5	11.1	25.6	43
Japan [5]	2007	28.3	5.5	19.6	40
Korea, Republic of	2007	26.5	4.4	16.7	35 [6]
Mexico	2007	18	...	...	28
Russia	2007	35.9	4.0	11.1	13
Saudi Arabia [7]	2008	6.7	...	...	...
South Africa	2007	30.9	8.5	27.3	40
Turkey	2007	23.7	4.0	17.0	35
United Kingdom	2007	36.1	10.9	30.1	40
United States	2007	28.3	10.8	38.1	35 [7]

Sources: www.bus.umich.edu/OTPR/otpr/OTPRdataV3.asp (The World Tax Database of the University of Michigan); KPMG (2008) database; PriceWaterhouseCoopers (2008); and IBFD (2008).

[1]General government.

[2]Includes withholding tax on wages and half the revenue of tax withheld on capital.

[3]Sum of the federal and provincial top marginal rates. Lowest rate corresponds to Alberta (flat 10 percent rate) and highest to Nova Scotia.

[4]Central government only.

[5]The rate is for PIT but revenue includes also the inhabitant tax composed of a 10 percent tax on income earned in the previous year and a poll tax.

[6]The rate will be reduced to 33 percent from 2012.

[7]Rate is for the federal PIT but revenue includes that of state and local PITs.

marginal rates of PIT. Incentive effects on the labor supply of primary workers are generally modest (Blundell and Macurdy, 1999) including for high earners: the substantial reduction in top marginal tax rates in Russia on movement to a flat tax of 13 percent, for instance, has been found to have small effects (Ivanova, Keen, and Klemm, 2005; Gorodnichenko, Martinez-Vasquez, and Peter, 2009). Tax effects on the participation decisions of secondary workers can be substantial, however, even at currently historically low levels of progressivity and top marginal tax rates (Table 3.7). Account needs to be taken also of high effective marginal rates implied by the withdrawal of benefits, including earned income tax credits; and better targeting of these, as discussed in Chapter 2, will amplify these effects. There is significant evidence that higher rates of PIT risk encourage tax avoidance (through the use of deductions, for example) and evasion, particularly for higher net income individuals (Saez, Slemrod, and Giertz, 2009). They are increasingly important as a source of revenue, reflecting increased inequality in recent years, making it natural to look to them for an increased contribution; but they also have a greater facility for avoidance (Box 3.1) making this difficult to do. Increased rates of social contributions, discussed earlier, can cause compliance difficulties at the lower end of the income distribution, but this can be addressed, in part, by integrating tax and social contribution administrations.

There is a significant scope in some countries, however, for base-broadening and simplification within the PIT, which could raise substantial revenue. For example, Japan and Korea have relatively high top marginal PIT rates (respectively, 40 and 35 percent), but have relatively low PIT ratios (5.5 and 4.4 percent of GDP) compared to other advanced G-20 countries. Such reforms would likely improve equity, given the nature of many of the base narrowing provisions presently existing. And in some countries that are heavily reliant on the PIT and in need of large fiscal adjustment, there may be little choice but to raise intermediate marginal rates in the PIT schedule.

Other

Carbon pricing

Pricing greenhouse gas emissions—by taxing carbon or auctioning emissions permits—could raise large sums. Globally efficient pricing could raise US$50–660 billion annually,[53] increasing over the next decades as the efficient price rises faster than emissions falls. The completeness of coverage

[53]Global emissions are now around 11 billion tons of carbon (tC) per year, but estimates of their marginal social cost vary widely, from US$5–60 per ton. This is less than the figure for potential revenue from petroleum taxes noted in the discussion on excise taxes above, since although the base of a comprehensive carbon tax would be far wider than petroleum (which accounts for about 4 billion tC of emissions), petroleum fuel taxes cover externalities much broader than carbon emissions alone.

Box 3.1. Taxing High Net Income Individuals (HNIIs)

This is an area of growing importance and difficulty. Those with the highest incomes pay a substantial share of all PIT: the top 0.1 percent of taxpayers in Germany, for instance, pay 8 percent of PIT; and in the United States, the top 0.7 percent pays 37 percent. HNIIs account for an average of 20–25 percent of total PIT revenue among G-20 countries. At the same time, however, they pose significant risk of non-compliance: HNIIs draw a significant fraction of their income from sources offering great opportunities for avoidance and evasion, including non-cash compensation (bonuses, stock options, and fringe benefits), entrepreneurial income, and investment: in the United States, capital gains alone have accounted for about one third of total income for taxpayers at the top of the income spectrum. HNIIs often have access to off-shore investment vehicles, which can facilitate non-compliance. An estimated 7–16 percent of assets of those with high wealth are held offshore,[1] though this varies greatly by region (with roughly 30 percent of Latin American and Middle Eastern assets held offshore, but less than 5 percent in North America and Japan). Little is known about the revenue cost of the evasion and avoidance associated with HNIIs, but many tax administrations believe it to be substantial (and see signs of this in the encouraging results of voluntary disclosure initiatives discussed below). They are conscious too of the danger that perceptions of the richest not paying their "fair share" will erode compliance more widely.

Combating avoidance and evasion among HNIIs requires not only increased enforcement, but also anti-abuse legislation and addressing fundamental tax distortions. For example, a common way to shelter income is by using tax (but not economic) loss-generating schemes to offset other income: countries have responded to this by, for instance, disallowing use of passive losses to offset income and ignoring transactions without economic substance, but scope for game-playing remains. Tax planning by transforming one type of income into another—often recharacterizing ordinary income as (preferentially-treated) capital gains—is invited by applying sharply different tax rates to different types of receipts. A lower tax rate on all forms of capital income—as under a dual income tax—would mean both fewer resources wasted on tax planning and reduced incentives for cross-border evasion.

[1]OECD (2009c) defining "high net wealth individuals," (HNWIs) as individuals with at least US$1million in net investable, non-residential assets.

(by country and emission source) this presumes is unachievable in the near term, but realistic short-term sums are still substantial. Current legislative proposals for emissions trading in the United States have revenue potential of about US$870 billion over 2011–19: roughly US$100 billion annually, or ½ percent of GDP—15 percent of the cumulative forecast fiscal deficit for that period (Congressional Budget Office, 2009a, b). Revenues from such schemes might appropriately be reduced by compensating poor consumers and some offsetting of fuel and other taxes; and their cross-country allocation will depend on arrangements for trading emissions rights (IMF, 2008). Nevertheless, carbon pricing provides a clear opportunity for substantially increasing revenue while enhancing efficiency and sustainable growth.

Realizing these gains requires limiting the free allocation of permits and extending the scope of carbon pricing. Around two-thirds of the potential revenue (from 2013–20) from schemes proposed in the EU, the United States, and Australia, is forgone under current plans to award almost all permits free of charge, conferring large windfall profits.[54] Swift transition to full auctioning[55] could raise hundreds of billions of dollars. Revenue (and efficiency) would also be enhanced by broadening the base of carbon pricing. There is little economic rationale, in particular, for the current exclusion of international transportation fuels not merely from carbon pricing but from any fuel excise:[56] taxing them could generate US$150–200 billion over the coming decade in the G-20, though substantial international coordination would again be required.

Property taxes

Property taxes[57] are a promising source of increased revenue for some countries, but there are practical obstacles. They currently yield around 3 percent of GDP in Canada, the United Kingdom, and the United States, but well below 1 percent in other G-20 countries. Efficiency and fairness argue strongly for firm use of property taxes: they are relatively benign for growth; raise few issues of international coordination; and, while their incidence is still not fully understood (Sennoga, Sjoquist, and Wallace, 2008), they seem to be borne mainly by the well-off. Obstacles to their wider use include administrative complexities and costs (including the development of efficient cadastre and valuation mechanisms), and the unpopularity that their transparency can bring. The (appropriate) assignment of property taxes predominantly to lower levels of government may pose challenges for increased revenue raising. This, though, is another area with clear potential for significant and relatively efficient medium-term revenue enhancement in several countries.

---

[54]Rate-of-return regulations, as for some utility companies in the United States, may limit such windfalls.

[55]For example, efforts to increase auctioning to industrial producers in the EU (from 30 percent in 2013 to 80 percent by 2020) have been blunted by special provisions for firms exposed to risks of "carbon leakage."

[56]Keen and Strand (2007) assess the case for taxing international aviation.

[57]The focus here is on recurrent immovable property taxes.

Improving Tax Compliance[58]

Significant tax gaps are widespread in the G-20. VAT compliance gaps (the difference between actual and potential VAT revenues) are 20 percent in some (Mexico, Italy, and some other EU countries), but nearer to 10 percent in others (France and Germany). Compliance is generally very high for income taxes withheld or subject to third-party reporting, but for other sources of income is commonly very low: for small traders, for instance, the gap is over 50 percent in the United States. Improving revenue administration and combating tax abuse could yield considerable revenue—the discussion on value added taxes above estimates that extra revenue equivalent to 0.8 percent of GDP could be collected by reducing the VAT gap in G-20 countries in the coming years.

Pervasive tax abuse significantly erodes revenue through:

- *Informality*—estimates of the size of the informal economy in high-income countries range from 8–30 percent of GDP (Schneider, 2009);
- *Aggressive tax planning*—contrived schemes pushing the boundaries of legal interpretation;
- *Offshore tax abuse*—evasion and avoidance through tax havens and bank secrecy jurisdictions;[59]
- *Tax fraud*—mostly through false tax refund and credit claims, including by organized crime: EU VAT fraud losses, for instance, were estimated to be $80–$140 billion in 2006 (International VAT Association, 2007); and
- *Unpaid tax debts*—weak payment compliance and enforcement, resulting in large stocks of tax debt.

The crisis has aggravated compliance problems;[60] restoring tax discipline is an immediate priority. For example, in the United Kingdom, the VAT gap increased by 3 percentage points between 2007–08 and 2008–09, and Lithuania's VAT debt more than doubled in the first half of 2009. Taxpayers who have drifted towards informality need to be brought back into the system, and there may be a resurgence of contrived tax schemes as the

---

[58]Harrison and others (forthcoming) further develops the content of this section.

[59]Offshore tax abuse ranges from blatant tax evasion (hiding money in secret offshore bank accounts) to use of complex and opaque structures by corporations to artificially shift income into low-tax jurisdictions.

[60]See Brondolo (2009); and also Sancak, Velloso, and Xing (2010).

appetite for risk increases and corporations seek to restore their financial positions. Revenue agencies must be alert to new schemes, such as abuse of the very substantial tax losses emerging from the crisis—$1.1 trillion of bank losses and write-downs have been reported (OECD, 2009c).

Pressure to reduce tax gaps presents an opportunity to improve revenue administration and tax compliance through medium-term systemic solutions. Improving the medium-term fiscal position requires reshaping revenue administration. There are four priorities: *intensifying international collaboration*, especially in exchanging tax information; *developing sound risk-based compliance strategies*; *strengthening legal frameworks*, including the powers of revenue agencies (e.g., in accessing information and conducting audits); and *exploiting new information technology* to better align tax compliance management with businesses' lifecycles.

Recent advances in international collaboration in tax information exchange and transparency are an important step forward—but implementation is critical and further opportunities remain for stronger cooperation. Recognizing the need for more global responses, the G-20 has enhanced its support of OECD efforts to establish international standards of tax information exchange and transparency. This has resulted in a large increase in the number of bilateral tax information exchange agreements with bank secrecy and tax haven jurisdictions. Continued international resolve and cooperation will be necessary to ensure that commitments under the agreements are met; technical assistance may need to be provided to tax havens to improve their administrative capacity and legal frameworks to facilitate timely information exchange. The need for stronger cross-country collaboration is evident in other areas too, for example, to be more effective in responding to criminal fraud. The EU has recognized that lack of collaboration between Member States has contributed to the vulnerabilities exploited by a raft of multi-billion dollar intra-community VAT frauds and, more recently, frauds associated with the trading of carbon credit permits. Improved systems of information exchange between EU revenue agencies would enhance early warning of emerging revenue risks; joint investigations should be expanded. Cross-country alignment of more effective domestic responses to cross-border evasion (such as through voluntary disclosure compliance programs—discussed below) should be also pursued.

Fundamental strengthening of compliance improvement strategies is crucial. Driven by risk management approaches, this entails:

- *Efficient gathering and administration of taxpayer and third-party information* utilizing modern technology and streamlined processes to reduce compliance costs and facilitate modeling of revenue risks during all stages of the taxpayer's business lifecycle;
- *Robust revenue analysis and identification of emerging compliance risks*; and [61]
- *Development of appropriate responses to mitigate identified risks*—mitigation strategies will vary depending on the underlying reasons for non-compliance. For example, audits and penalties are a fitting response to deliberate evasion, while education and assistance are appropriate to situations where taxpayers do not understand the law. Importantly, mitigation strategies should seek to achieve wide impact and enduring compliance within the broader taxpaying community.

In emerging economies—where, as discussed earlier, revenue possibilities from sustainable compliance improvement are greater—tackling endemic tax abuses to enhance the taxpaying culture requires significant capacity building in core systems of revenue administration (including in compliance-related areas of risk management, audit, collection enforcement, taxpayer services, and dispute resolution).[62] Through comprehensive reform efforts, revenue agencies in emerging economies can play an important role in fostering formalization, by helping new entrepreneurs and taking visible enforcement action against the shadow economy to establish tax discipline. In advanced economies, where systems of administration are more robust, the central compliance challenge is more about combating aggressive tax planning, offshore evasion, and tax fraud. These compliance risks require domestic and global responses and often novel approaches, like the recent voluntary disclosure programs aimed at bringing taxpayers involved in offshore tax abuse into compliance. These programs are an integral part of wider strategies to achieve enduring tax compliance; their success rests on large scale financial information gathering by revenue agencies, enhanced detection capabilities, and a commitment by the authorities to follow through with strong enforcement action, including prosecution, against those who choose

[61]The lack of in-depth analysis of revenue trends and risks by several G-20 countries imposes limitations on their capacity to manage compliance effectively, including compliance associated with sizeable tax expenditures. Few G-20 countries publish tax gap and tax expenditure estimates; in many, there is insufficient involvement by the tax administration in estimating, analyzing and controlling compliance of tax expenditures.

[62]Appendix 8 describes the characteristics of modern tax administration. The IMF Fiscal Affairs Department provides technical assistance to IMF member countries to support their efforts in modernizing tax and customs administrations.

to continue cheating the tax system.[63] Unlike voluntary disclosure programs, traditional tax amnesties in some countries have focused on short-term repatriation of revenues, without enhancing the compliance management capabilities of their revenue agencies and promoting sustainable compliance improvement. Tax amnesties have sometimes been implemented through anonymous one-off payments (normally a fixed fee) via the banking system, without provision of information to tax administrations, and no-questions-asked policies that preclude future audits of tax years covered under these amnesties.

Legal frameworks need to be enhanced to address compliance risks and pervasive tax abuse:

- *Countries can do more within existing tax and financial regulatory structures*—making the most of existing legal powers, data and intelligence in relation to financial flows requires the highest levels of cooperation and information exchange between revenue agencies and corporate regulators, banking supervisors, anti-money laundering regulators, financial intelligence units, border management and other law enforcement agencies.
- *Further legislative solutions need to be adopted to combat offshore tax abuse*—it may be appropriate to impose stronger domestic sanctions and other disincentives (e.g., stiff fines and criminal prosecution of evasion and its facilitation; and policy measures to discourage transactions with uncooperative low tax jurisdictions, such as introducing withholding taxes on funds sent offshore and denying certain expense deductions).
- *Aggressive tax planning needs to be tackled with firm countermeasures, including development of common good practice in anti-avoidance rules*—an effective set of general anti-avoidance rules should be available to revenue agencies as part of the tax litigation armory. Development of a model set of principles—based on best practice[64]—to guide all G-20 countries in the drafting of effective general anti-avoidance rules would be a major step forward. Procedural rules should also be developed to assure that taxpayers cannot avoid scrutiny of their questionable transactions by

[63]Ireland has collected €2.6 billion in delinquent taxes over recent years applying these programs—0.3 percent of GDP was collected from voluntary disclosures in 2005 alone; further substantial amounts were recovered through subsequent enforcement actions—Hart (forthcoming) analyzes voluntary disclosure programs in several countries, including Canada, France, Germany, the United Kingdom, and the United States.

[64]Experience in countries that have a strong general anti avoidance rule in the tax law (e.g., Australia) indicates that this approach is a more effective deterrent than reliance on remedies not embodied in the law.

playing the audit lottery. These might include mandatory disclosure of specifically identified transactions or, more generally, uncertain tax positions that put significant amounts of revenue at risk. Domestic and international codes of tax practice for banks, other large corporations and tax intermediaries—with appropriate incentives to comply—should also be pursued. Strong penalties for promoters, facilitators, and users of contrived and opaque tax schemes should be adopted.

- *Tax litigation needs to be streamlined*—good practices in negotiated settlements can also minimize instances of costly and lengthy litigation.

Intensifying the use of modern information technology in delivering revenue administration will significantly improve compliance management and reduce compliance costs. Besides basic internet-based services (e.g., tax information and return filing) widely adopted in several countries, revenue agencies should intensify the adoption of electronic solutions to automate and align economic agents' tax compliance and business cycles. Good examples of this direction include on-line taxpayers' registration and termination of business, automatic gathering of third-party information, business-to-government standard financial reporting as a by-product of natural business processes, and use of electronic invoices with the potential of real-time transaction monitoring and verification of VAT compliance. There are also other successful technology-based innovations that could be adopted more widely including, for example, automated risk-based selection systems, on-line auction of seized assets, pre-populated tax returns, on-line compliance reporting services, and accounting systems for promoting formalization of small taxpayers. The opportunities presented by these and other technological solutions, in a context of the key directions discussed earlier to enhance international transparency and strengthen compliance management, pave the way to reshaping revenue administration to meet the compliance challenges of the digital age and globalized economy.

APPENDIX

1 Primary Expenditure Trends

Figure A.1. Advanced G-20 General Government Primary Expenditure Trends 1990–2008: Economic Classification

(In percent of GDP)

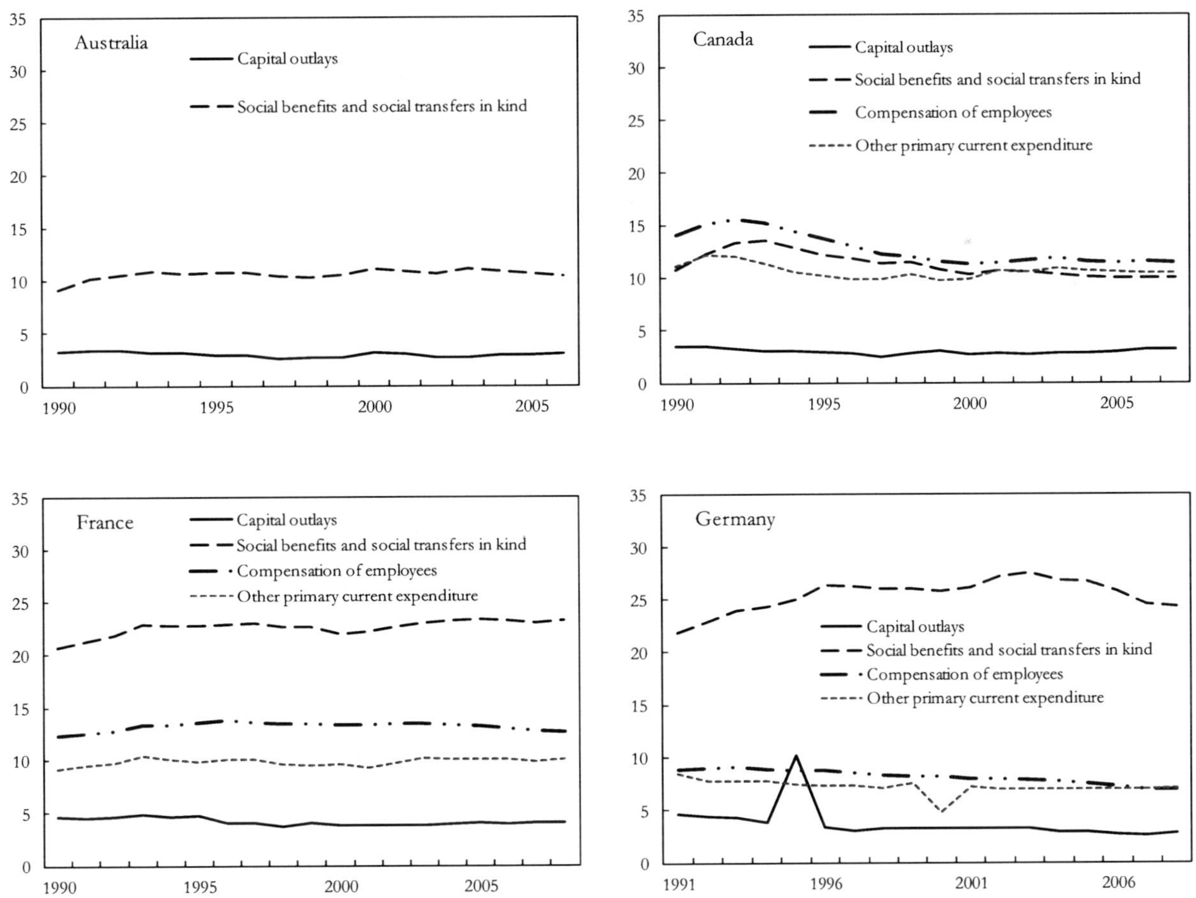

Figure A.1 *(concluded)*

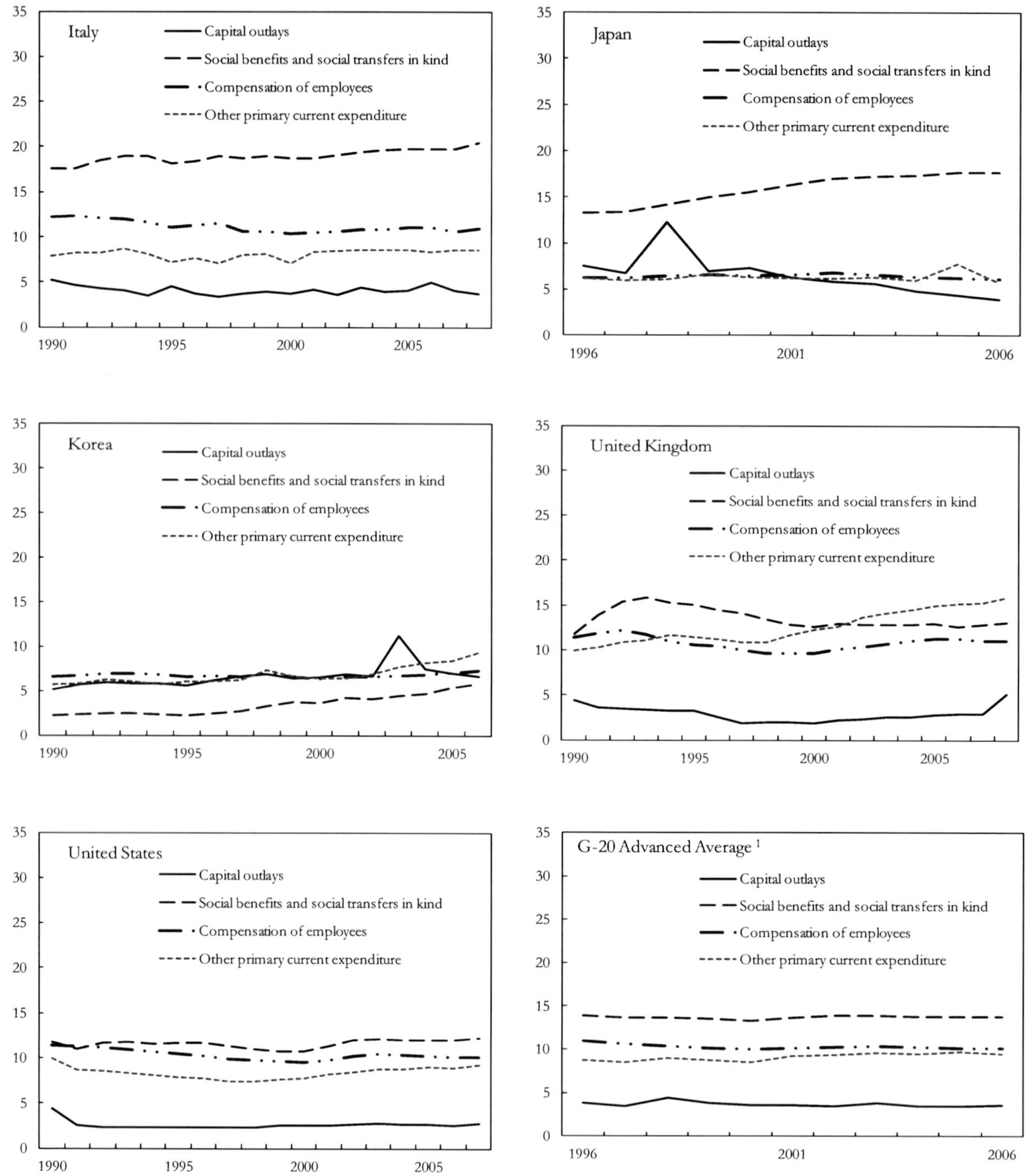

Sources: Eurostat; and OECD.

Figure A.2. Advanced G-20 General Government Primary Expenditure Trends, 1997–2008: Functional Classification

(In percent of GDP)

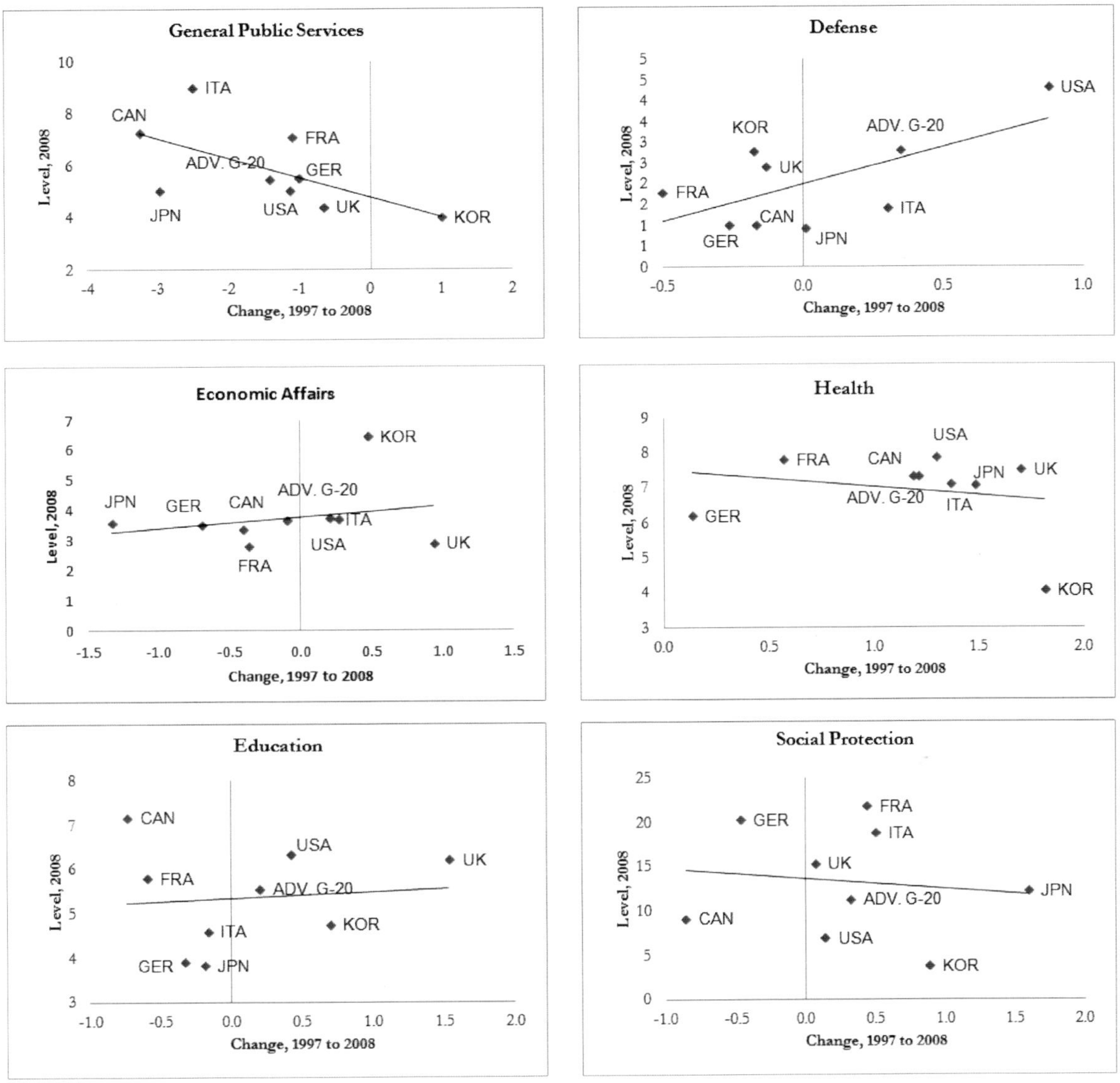

Figure A.2 *(concluded)*

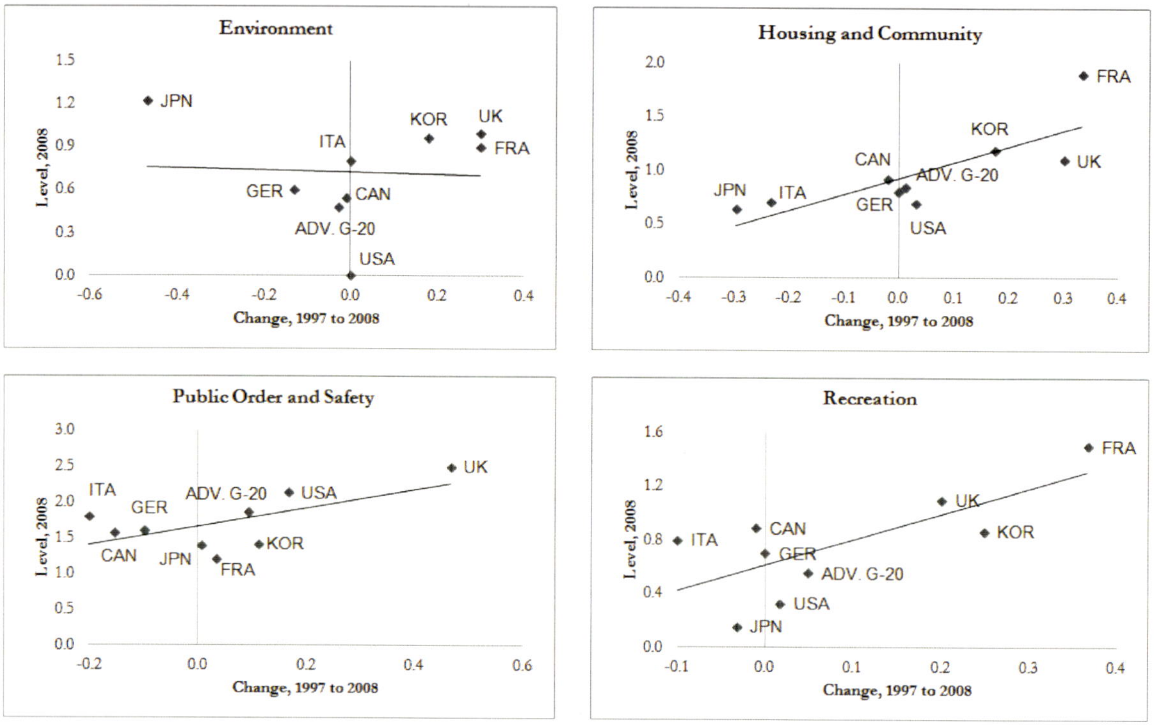

Sources: OECD; and Eurostat.

Notes: Or latest year available; averages are PPP GDP weighted.

Figure A.3. Emerging G-20 Primary Public Expenditure Trends, 1995–2008: Economic Classification

(In percent of GDP)

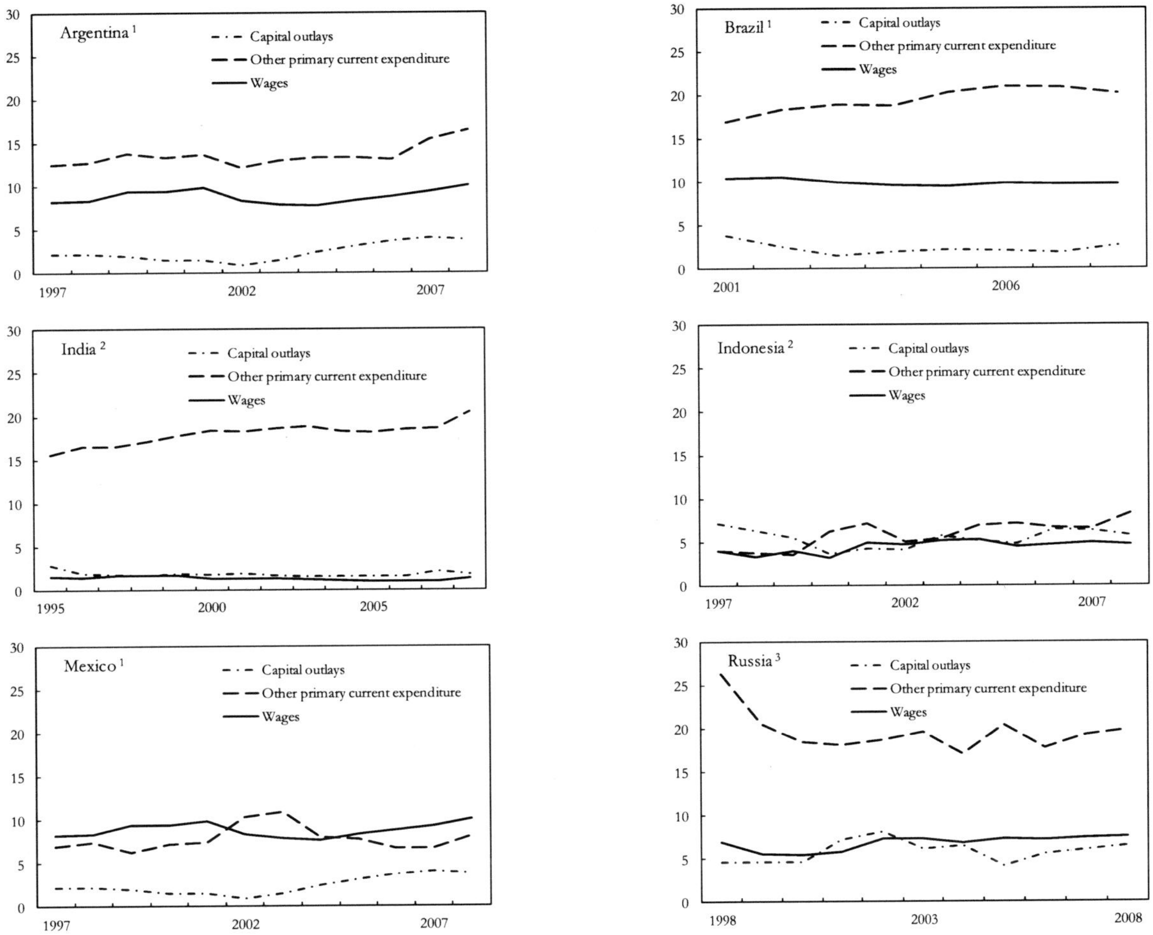

Figure A.3 *(concluded)*

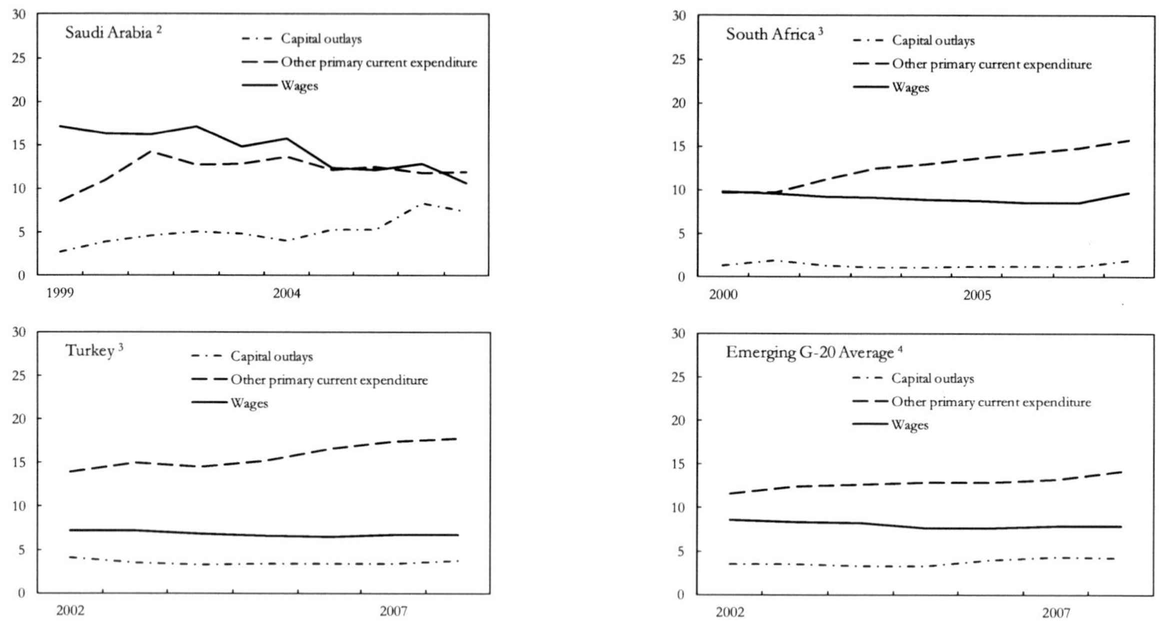

Sources: WEO; and IMF staff estimates.

[1]Nonfinancial public sector.

[2]Central government.

[3]General government.

[4]PPP GDP weighted.

APPENDIX

2 Country Experience with Large Adjustments

Table A.1. Country Experiences with Large Fiscal Adjustment: Economic Classification and Age-Related Spending

(In percent of GDP)

Country (end-year)	Length (years)	Size of adjustment	*of which: Primary expenditure*	*Of which: economic classification* Compensation of employees	Social benefits and social transfers in kind	Gross fixed capital formation	Other	*Of which: age-related* Health	Pensions	of which: Old age pensions	of which: Survivor pensions
Ireland (1989)	11	20.0	-11.8	...	...	...	...	-2.3	-0.4	-0.3	-0.1
Sweden (2000)	7	13.3	-10.4	-2.0	-4.1	-1.2	-3.1	-0.1	-1.3	-1.2	-0.1
Finland (2000)	7	13.3	-10.7	-2.7	-7.2	-0.5	-0.3	-0.7	-1.5	-1.3	-0.2
Sweden (1987)	7	12.5	-5.3	...	...	...	...	-0.8	0.6	0.6	0.0
Denmark (1986)	4	12.3	-6.0	-2.7	-2.5	-0.5	-0.3	-0.6	-0.4	-0.3	-0.1
Greece (1995)	6	12.1	-2.3	...	...	...	...	0.9	-0.3	-0.2	-0.1
Israel (1983)	3	11.1	-11.2	...	...	...	...	...	...	...	...
Belgium (1998)	15	11.1	-10.7	-0.7	-1.0	-1.2	-7.8	0.7	0.0	0.8	-0.8
Canada (1999)	14	10.4	-6.4	-2.4	0.6	-0.5	-4.1	-0.1	0.6	0.5	0.1
Cyprus (2007)	4	8.5	-0.7	-1.3	0.1	-0.5	1.0	...	...	...	...
United Kingdom (2000)	7	8.3	-5.1	-1.2	-2.7	-0.9	-0.2	0.0	-0.2	-0.1	-0.1
Japan (1990)	12	8.1	-1.1	...	...	...	...	-0.2	0.3	0.4	-0.1
Italy (1993)	8	7.9	1.0	0.7	2.0	-0.8	-0.9	0.8	0.0	0.1	-0.1
Portugal (1985)	4	7.5	0.8	...	...	...	...	0.0	0.3	0.2	0.1
Luxembourg (1985)	4	6.9	-1.4	...	...	...	...	-0.2	-0.7	-0.5	-0.2
Luxembourg (2001)	10	6.7	-1.6	-0.9	1.4	-0.1	-2.0	0.5	-2.0	-3.2	1.2
Iceland (2006)	4	6.3	-1.6	-0.6	-0.9	-0.5	0.5	-0.8	-0.1	-0.1	0.0
Netherlands (2000)	10	6.3	-9.0	-1.2	-6.4	0.0	-1.4	-0.6	-1.6	-1.0	-0.6
Denmark (2005)	11	5.9	-3.8	0.2	-3.1	0.0	-0.9	1.3	-1.1	-1.1	0.0
Hong Kong SAR (2005)	4	5.8	-1.5	...	...	...	...	...	...	...	...
Australia (1988)	4	5.8	-5.1	...	-0.9	-0.8	...	-0.3	-0.2	0.1	-0.3
New Zealand (1995)	4	5.8	-7.1	-1.5	-1.6	0.4	-4.2	-0.5	-4.2	-2.8	-1.4
Austria (2001)	6	5.8	-4.6	-2.5	0.3	-1.7	-0.8	0.7	0.2	0.2	0.0
Iceland (2000)	6	5.7	-0.7	2.2	-2.1	-0.3	-0.5	0.7	-0.1	-0.1	0.0
United States (2000)	8	5.7	-2.6	-1.4	-1.1	0.2	-0.4	0.0	-0.4	-0.3	-0.1
Germany (2000)	9	5.3	-1.9	-1.0	2.9	-1.0	-2.8	-0.1	1.1	1.1	0.0
Germany (1989)	10	5.3	-5.4	...	...	...	...	-0.3	-0.4	-0.1	-0.3
Switzerland (2000)	7	5.2	-0.6	-0.6	0.3	-0.6	0.2	0.5	0.2	0.2	0.0
Cyprus (1994)	3	5.2	-0.9	...	...	...	...	...	...	...	...
Spain (2006)	11	5.2	-2.7	-1.2	-1.5	0.6	-0.6	0.40	-1.0	-0.6	-0.4
Mean	7.6	8.3	-4.2	-1.1	-1.4	-0.5	-1.5	0.0	-0.5	-0.3	-0.1
G-20	9.1	7.0	-3.9	-1.5	-0.2	-0.6	-1.9	-0.1	0.1	0.2	-0.1
Median	7.0	6.8	-3.2	-1.2	-1.0	-0.5	-0.8	-0.1	-0.3	-0.1	-0.1

Sources: WEO; Eurostat; and OECD.

Note: Data reflect both cyclical and structural factors; averages are unweighted.

Table A.2. Country Experiences with Large Adjustment: Functional Classification

(In percent of GDP)

Country (end-year)	Length (years)	Size of adjustment	of which: Total expenditure	Of which: General public services	Defense	Public order and safety	Economic affairs	Environment protection	Housing and community amenities	Health	Recreation, culture, and religion	Education	Social protection
Ireland (1989)	11	20.0	-14.4	-0.6	-0.6	...	-5.4	...	-1.1	-2.2	-0.1	-1.1	-1.6
Sweden (2000)	7	13.3	-9.5	-1.2	-0.1	-0.1	-1.8	0.1	-1.9	0.0	-0.7	-0.2	-3.4
Finland (2000)	7	13.3	-15.5	-1.2	-0.7	-0.1	-4.0	0.0	-0.2	-0.5	0.0	-0.9	-8.1
Sweden (1987)	7	12.5	-9.3	0.5	-0.4	-0.2	-4.1	...	-2.1	0.5	0.0	-1.0	-5.4
Denmark (1986)	4	12.3	-4.7	-0.5	-0.5	...	-0.7	...	-0.4	0.0	-0.1	-0.8	-1.9
Greece (1995)	6	12.1	-6.2	-1.0	-0.8	-0.1	-0.8	...	0.1	-0.8	-0.1	-0.1	-0.1
Israel (1983)	3	11.1	15.3	0.0	-5.9	0.0	3.6	...	0.0	0.7	0.1	-0.8	0.9
Belgium (1998)	15	11.1	...	...	...	...	...	...	...	...	...	...	...
Canada (1999)	14	10.4	-3.6	-0.7	-0.6	...	-2.4	...	-0.1	-1.3	0.1	-0.4	1.3
Cyprus (2007)	4	8.5	-2.1	-0.2	-0.4	-0.2	-1.4	0.0	0.0	-0.5	0.1	-0.2	0.4
United Kingdom (2000)	7	8.3	-5.7	-0.7	-0.8	-0.1	-1.1	0.1	-0.5	0.1	0.0	0.2	-2.9
Japan (1990)	12	8.1	...	...	...	...	...	...	...	...	...	...	...
Italy (1993)	8	7.9	...	...	...	...	...	...	...	...	...	...	...
Portugal (1985)	4	7.5	...	...	...	...	...	...	...	...	...	...	...
Luxembourg (1985)	4	6.9	-0.5	-0.1	0.0	...	-0.1	...	0.0	0.0	0.0	0.0	-0.3
Luxembourg (2001)	10	6.7	-1.9	0.4	-0.3	0.2	-3.0	0.0	-0.3	0.2	0.3	0.0	0.8
Iceland (2006)	4	6.3	-3.4	-0.8	0.0	-0.1	-0.8	0.0	0.0	-0.6	-0.2	0.1	-0.8
Netherlands (2000)	10	6.3	...	...	...	...	...	...	...	...	...	...	...
Denmark (2005)	11	5.9	-6.4	-4.0	-0.3	0.0	-0.7	0.0	-0.1	0.1	0.0	0.5	-2.0
Hong Kong SAR (2005) 3/	4	5.8	...	...	...	...	...	...	...	...	...	...	...
Australia (1988)	4	5.8	-1.9	0.1	-0.3	-0.2	-0.6	...	0.0	0.9	0.0	-0.2	-0.8
New Zealand (1995)	4	5.8	...	...	...	...	...	...	...	...	...	...	...
Austria (2001)	6	5.8	-4.4	-1.2	-0.1	-0.1	0.3	-0.9	-0.3	-1.1	0.0	-0.2	-0.8
Iceland (2000)	6	5.7	39.5	0.3	...	0.1	-1.6	...	-0.2	0.8	0.0	0.9	-0.5
United States (2000)	8	5.7	-3.8	-1.1	-1.5	0.1	-0.2	0.0	-0.2	-0.1	0.0	0.2	-1.1
Germany (2000)	9	5.3	-2.1	-0.7	-0.6	0.1	-3.4	-0.3	0.1	0.1	0.0	-0.3	2.9
Germany (1989)	10	5.3	0.1	-0.2	-0.4	...	0.0	...	0.0	-0.2	0.0	-0.1	-0.2
Switzerland (2000)	7	5.2	-0.2	0.0	-0.4	0.0	-0.3	...	0.0	-0.3	0.0	-0.1	0.0
Cyprus (1994)	3	5.2	-3.1	-0.3	0.1	-0.2	0.5	...	0.2	0.0	0.0	0.3	0.6
Spain (2006)	11	5.2	-4.7	-2.9	-0.2	-0.1	0.1	0.1	-0.1	0.3	0.1	-0.3	-1.6
Mean	7.3	8.6	-4.9	-0.8	-0.4	-0.1	-1.4	-0.1	-0.3	-0.3	0.0	-0.2	-1.2
G-20	8.7	6.8	-2.8	-0.5	-0.7	0.0	-1.3	-0.1	-0.1	-0.1	0.0	-0.1	-0.1
Median	7.0	6.7	-3.8	-0.7	-0.4	-0.1	-0.8	0.0	-0.1	0.0	0.0	-0.2	-0.8

Sources: WEO; Eurostat; GFS; and OECD.

Note: Data reflect both cyclical and structural factors; averages are unweighted.

APPENDIX

3 Pension Spending Projections, 2010–2050

Methodology for Projecting Pensions

Projections for public pensions reflect official projections where available (see sources below). For countries where official projections are not available, the following assumptions are made: (i) constant coverage ratio of pensioners to population aged above 65 years and constant replacement rate; and (ii) changes are driven by employment ratio and old-age dependency ratio. Demographic projections are based on projections from the European Commission (2009) and U.S. Bureau of Census. Economic projections are broadly based on the convergence criteria assumed in the European Commission's Ageing Report, 2009, and staff estimates of labor participation rates.

Sources:

- European countries: European Commission Ageing Report (2009); for Cyprus, staff calculations of the recent reform;
- Australia: Productivity Commission (2005);
- New Zealand: New Zealand Treasury (2009);
- United States: Congressional Budget Office Report on Social Security (2009);
- Canada: CPP and QPP Actuarial Reports (2006);
- Japan: Ministry of Health, Labor and Welfare, 2009 Actuarial Report on Pensions; and

Table A.3. Pension Expenditures, 2010–50

(In percent of GDP)

	2010	2015	2020	2030	2040	2050	Change, 2010 to 2030	NPV of 2011-2030 spending Increase	NPV of 2031-2050 spending Increase
Advanced economies:									
Australia	3.1	3.4	3.7	4.3	4.6	4.8	1.2	11.8	22.3
Austria	12.7	12.8	13.0	13.8	13.9	14.0	1.1	7.6	18.1
Belgium	10.3	10.9	11.8	13.9	14.6	14.7	3.6	30.2	62.2
Canada	4.7	5.1	5.6	6.3	6.1	5.9	1.6	15.2	20.6
Cyprus	6.9	7.8	8.9	10.8	12.8	15.5	3.9	27.8	76.0
Czech Republic	7.1	6.9	6.9	7.1	8.4	10.2	0.0	-2.3	21.2
Denmark	9.4	10.2	10.6	10.6	10.4	9.6	1.2	17.0	12.5
Finland	10.7	11.8	12.6	13.9	13.6	13.3	3.2	33.4	43.2
France	13.5	13.5	13.6	14.2	14.4	14.2	0.7	3.9	12.6
Germany	10.2	10.1	10.5	11.5	12.1	12.3	1.3	7.6	27.1
Greece	11.6	12.2	13.2	17.1	21.4	24.0	5.5	37.6	141.2
Iceland	4.0	4.4	5.0	6.0	6.6	6.9	2.1	18.6	38.0
Ireland	4.1	4.3	4.6	5.4	6.4	8.0	1.3	10.3	35.8
Italy	14.0	14.0	14.1	14.8	15.6	14.7	0.8	3.7	18.3
Japan	10.3	10.8	10.6	10.1	10.7	11.0	-0.2	2.6	4.0
Korea	0.6	0.8	1.2	2.2	3.4	4.4	1.7	12.9	41.6
Luxembourg	8.6	8.9	9.9	14.2	18.4	22.1	5.6	36.3	146.8
Malta	8.3	9.1	9.3	9.3	10.5	12.0	1.0	14.3	33.4
Netherlands	6.5	7.2	7.8	9.3	10.3	10.3	2.8	24.4	53.4
New Zealand	4.7	4.8	5.3	6.7	7.7	8.0	2.0	13.1	41.8
Norway	9.6	10.8	11.5	12.7	13.4	13.3	3.1	32.4	54.1
Portugal	11.9	12.1	12.4	12.6	12.5	13.3	0.7	8.0	10.9
Slovakia	6.6	6.3	6.3	7.3	8.3	9.4	0.7	0.3	25.6
Slovenia	10.1	10.6	11.1	13.3	16.1	18.2	3.2	23.1	87.3
Spain	8.9	9.2	9.5	10.8	13.2	15.5	1.9	14.0	64.3
Sweden	9.6	9.5	9.4	9.5	9.4	9.0	-0.1	-2.5	-4.3
United Kingdo	6.7	6.8	6.9	7.6	8.0	8.1	0.9	5.8	17.7
United States	4.9	4.9	5.3	6.0	6.0	5.7	1.1	8.3	15.6
Emerging market economies:									
Argentina	5.9	5.7	5.6	6.3	7.2	8.6	0.4	-0.9	21.1
Brazil	8.5	8.4	8.4	9.8	12.8	15.8	1.3	2.5	64.9
Bulgaria	9.1	8.6	8.4	8.6	9.5	10.8	-0.5	-9.8	7.3
China	2.2	2.2	2.3	2.4	2.5	2.6	0.2	1.3	6.3
Estonia	6.4	6.2	5.9	5.6	5.4	5.3	-0.8	-7.8	-15.0
Hungary	11.3	10.9	11.0	11.0	12.2	13.2	-0.3	-5.7	12.1
India	1.7	2.0	2.1	2.1	1.7	0.9	0.4	6.8	-1.0
Indonesia	0.9	0.9	1.1	1.3	1.7	2.1	0.4	3.2	11.2

Table A.3 *(concluded)*

	2010	2015	2020	2030	2040	2050	Change, 2010 to 2030	NPV of 2011-2030 spending Increase	NPV of 2031-2050 spending Increase
Latvia	5.1	4.8	5.2	5.9	6.1	5.8	0.8	3.2	13.1
Lithuania	6.5	6.5	6.9	8.2	9.1	10.4	1.7	10.8	39.9
Malaysia	2.9	3.3	3.7	4.6	5.2	5.6	1.7	15.0	32.5
Mexico	2.4	3.1	3.4	4.5	4.6	3.5	2.1	19.2	30.2
Pakistan	1.4	1.3	1.4	1.8	2.1	2.6	0.4	2.1	11.8
Philippines	1.1	1.2	1.3	1.6	1.8	2.0	0.5	4.0	10.6
Poland	10.8	9.6	9.7	9.4	9.2	9.1	-1.4	-18.9	-23.5
Romania	8.4	8.5	8.8	10.4	12.6	14.8	2.0	11.6	62.7
Russia	5.1	5.1	5.8	7.5	8.3	10.2	2.5	31.5	94.9
Saudi Arabia	2.2	2.4	2.7	3.6	4.9	7.1	1.4	10.0	43.0
South Africa	1.3	1.4	1.6	1.9	2.1	2.3	0.6	5.2	11.5
Turkey	4.9	5.6	7.0	8.9	10.5	15.4	4.0	22.1	48.2
Ukraine	12.8	13.6	15.2	18.8	20.9	24.2	6.0	49.3	123.3
Average	5.9	6.1	6.3	7.0	7.4	7.8	1.0	8.3	23.2
Advanced	7.4	7.6	7.9	8.5	8.9	9.0	1.1	8.7	21.4
Emerging	3.7	3.8	4.0	4.6	5.1	5.8	1.0	7.8	25.9
G20	5.6	5.7	5.9	6.5	6.9	7.1	0.9	7.7	20.4
Advanced	7.1	7.2	7.5	8.1	8.3	8.3	0.9	7.3	16.7
Emerging	3.2	3.3	3.6	4.2	4.7	5.3	1.0	8.2	26.1

Sources: Country authorities; European Commission (2009); OECD (2009e); ILO(2010); and IMF staff estimates.

Note: The net present value (NPV) of future pension spending increases is measured as the NPV of the deviation of pension expenditures as a percentage point of GDP from their 2010 level. The discount rate used is 1 percent a year in excess of GDP growth for each country.

- Others: Staff projections using ILO (2010), IMF, World Bank documents and country authorities estimates.

Data Sources:

- Population Projections: European Commission and U.S. Bureau of Census; and
- Employment Ratio: World Economic Outlook.

Table A.4. Statutory Retirement Ages and Life Expectancy at Retirement

	Earliest eligibility age for pension benefits, 2010	Statutory retirement age, 2010	Life expectancy after statutory retirement age, 2010	Increase in statutory retirment age by 2030 (planned or legislated)	Life expectancy after statutory retirement age, 2030
Advanced economies:					
Australia	65.0	65.0	17.4	2.0	19.2
Austria	60.0	65.0	17.9		18.6
Belgium	60.0	65.0	17.7		19.4
Canada	60.0	65.0	18.2		20.0
Cyprus	63.0	65.0	14.3		16.7
Czech Republic	58.8	61.8	18.8	3.2	22.0
Denmark	60.0	65.0	16.5	2.0	18.5
Finland	58.0	65.0	16.4		19.6
France	56.0	60.0	22.9		24.8
Germany	63.0	65.0	18.3	2.0	19.1
Greece	55.0	65.0	17.7		19.5
Iceland	60.0	67.0	15.4		16.9
Ireland	65.0	65.0	16.0		17.9
Italy	58.0	65.0	18.4		19.5
Japan	60.0	65.0	18.0		21.5
Korea	55.0	60.0	19.8	5.0	23.0
Luxembourg	57.0	65.0	17.8		18.7
Malta	61.0	61.0	19.6	4.0	23.6
Netherlands	65.0	65.0	15.9	2.0	18.3
New Zealand	65.0	65.0	17.3		18.6
Norway	67.0	67.0	15.2		16.6
Portugal	45.0	65.0	17.6		19.4
Slovakia	60.0	62.0	18.9		21.3
Slovenia	62.5	62.5	19.0	0.5	21.3
Spain	61.0	65.0	17.8	2.0	19.2
Sweden	61.0	65.0	17.0		19.4
United Kingdo	65.0	65.0	17.4	1.0	18.7
United States	62.0	65.8	16.3	1.0	17.3
Emerging market economies:					
Argentina	60.0	65.0	16.6		18.5
Brazil	53.0	65.0	13.3		15.2
Bulgaria	63.0	63.0	16.5		20.2
China	50.0	60.0	18.1		19.2
Estonia	58.0	63.0	18.3		21.2
Hungary	60.0	62.0	18.6	3.0	21.5
India	50.0	58.0	18.2		20.1
Indonesia	55.0	55.0	22.6		24.6

Table A.4 *(concluded)*

	Earliest eligibility age for pension benefits, 2010	Statutory retirement age, 2010	Life expectancy after statutory retirement age, 2010	Increase in statutory retirment age by 2030 (planned or legislated)	Life expectancy after statutory retirement age, 2030
Latvia	60.0	62.0	18.9		21.1
Lithuania	62.5	62.5	21.1		22.3
Malaysia	55.0	55.0	22.9		25.1
Mexico	60.0	65.0	16.3		17.2
Pakistan	55.0	60.0	17.0		17.9
Philippines	55.0	60.0	17.4		19.4
Poland	60.0	65.0	16.1		19.1
Romania	58.3	63.3	16.9	1.8	19.2
Russia	50.0	60.0	21.1		22.9
Saudi Arabia	55.0	60.0	19.0		19.9
South Africa	61.0	61.0	16.4		19.8
Turkey	60.0	60.0	17.3		19.4
Ukraine	58.0	60.0	20.5		22.6
Average	58.9	63.0	17.9	0.6	19.9
Advanced	60.1	64.2	17.7	1.0	19.7
Emerging	57.1	61.2	18.2	0.2	20.3
G20	57.8	62.4	18.2	0.6	20.0
Advanced	60.4	64.0	18.5	1.2	20.3
Emerging	58.9	63.0	17.9	0.0	19.7

Sources: Country authorities; European Commission (2009); ILO (2010); UN (2008); OECD (2009e); Social Security Administration (2010); and IMF staff estimates.
Notes: Earliest eligibility age for pension benefits, including protected groups such as those in arduous or unhealthy employment that applies for new entrants to the labor force (some countries might have even earlier ages of eligibility for grandfathered groups). Legislated and planned increases in statutory retirement ages are included in the calculations for 2030.

APPENDIX

4 Pension Reform in the Advanced G-20

All advanced G-20 have undertaken reforms to stabilize pension finances. These reforms often included a combination of significant measures to increase revenues, raise statutory retirement ages, and reduce the generosity of benefits. Many of these changes come into effect beyond 2020. If implemented as legislated, these reforms are expected to largely offset the adverse effects of demographic developments, including through their effects on labor force participation rates—in the absence of reforms, pension spending in advanced G-20 countries would increase by 4½ percentage points of GDP to nearly 11½ percent of GDP in 2050 (Figure A.4). Nevertheless, pension spending is projected to rise from 7 percent of GDP in 2010 to 8½ percent in 2050. Reforms implemented by country were as follows:[65]

In **Australia,** the **2009 reform** envisaged a gradual increase in the statutory retirement age from 65 years to 67 years starting in 2017, and changed the income test by increasing the reduction in pensions from 40 cents to 50 cents for each dollar of non-pension income.

---

[65]See Ali Abbas and others (2010) for discussion of pension reforms in some European countries outside the G-20.

Figure A.4. Effects of Pension Reforms on Pension Expenditures in Advanced G-20 Countries, 2010–50

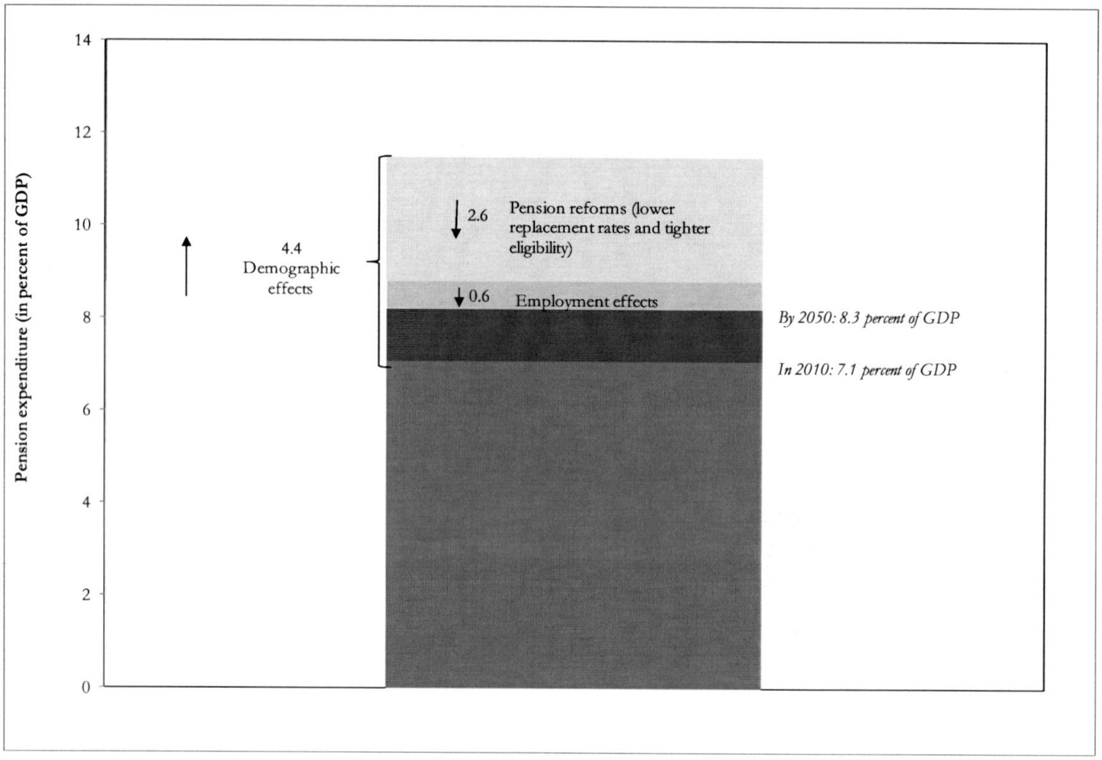

Source: IMF staff estimates.

In **Canada**, the contribution rate increased by 0.2 percent a year from 1987 to 1997. The **1997 reform** further raised it from 5.85 percent in 1997 to 9.9 percent in 2003 and reduced basic contribution holidays. Two stabilizing provisions were also introduced: (i) future increases in benefits are financed by increases in the contribution rate; and (ii) contribution rates and benefits indexation respond automatically to actuarial imbalances.

France increased the contribution rate from 4.7 to 6.55 for employees from 1985 to 1991. **The 1993 reform** increased the base wage for calculating pensions from the top 10 years to the top 25 years and changed the basis for calculating pensionable earnings from wages to prices. The minimum contribution period for a full pension increased from 37½ to 40 years. **The 2003 reform** linked the contribution years for a full pension to life expectancy. In the **early 1990s, Germany** changed the indexation of pensions from gross to net wages and tightened the requirements to receive a full pension before age 65 and increased the minimum age for early retirement after unemployment, after a transitional period, from 60 years to 63 years. The **2001 reform** included a privately funded second pillar and changed the formula to reduce benefits with increases in the contributions to the first and second pillars. The **2004 reform** introduced a "sustainability factor" to partially offset the effect of increases in the dependency ratio. In **2007,** the statutory retirement age was increased from 65 today to 67 after 2030.

In **Italy,** the **1992 reform** cut net pension liabilities by about 25 percent through (i) an increase in the retirement age for full benefits from 60 to 65 for men; (ii) an increase in reference earnings from 5 to 10 years (lifetime earnings for younger workers); (iii) a change in the basis of calculating pensionable earnings to prices plus 1 percent; (iv) an increase in contributing years for a full pension from 15 to 20 years; and (v) a change in indexation from wages to prices. The **1995 reform** adopted a Notional Defined Contribution system in which pensions depend on lifetime contributions and GDP growth. The **2004 reform** raised the minimum retirement age to 60 years with 35 years of contributions. In **2007,** the minimum retirement age was raised to reach 61 years in 2013.

In **Japan,** the **2004 reform** increased contributions rates for the employees' pension from 13.6 percent in 2005 to 18.3 percent in 2017. Benefits were reduced to offset the effects of a shrinking base of contributors and longer life expectancies. Earlier reforms changed the indexation of pensions from wages to prices, increased the retirement statutory to 65 years and extended the base of contributors to include employees 65 to 69 years.

In **Korea,** contribution rates were increased from 3 percent in 1988 to 6 percent in 1993 to 9 percent in 1998. The **1998 reform** cut replacement rates from 70 to 60 percent and raised the pensionable age from 60 to 65 years. The **2007 reform** stabilized contribution rates at 9 percent and reduced replacement rates from 60 percent in 2007 to 50 percent in 2008 to 40 percent in 2028. Contribution rates are set to increase further (from 9 percent) after 2010. The reform also expanded the basic pension from 5 percent of earnings in 2008 to 10 percent in 2028.

In the **United Kingdom**, the National Insurance Contribution rates have been generally increasing. The **2007 reform** raised the statutory retirement age from 65 in 2008 to 68 in 2027 (the pension age of women will be equalized by 2020). This reform also loosened eligibility for a full pension from about 44 years to 30 years.

In the **United States,** the **1983 reform** accelerated scheduled increases in the payroll tax to 12.4 percent of covered earnings after 1990, levied taxes on social security benefits and raised the statutory retirement age from 65 years to 67 years in 2027. It also expanded the base of participants to include federal employees.

APPENDIX

5 Policy Reforms to Close Pension Deficit

Changes in pension expenditures (*PE*) in percent of GDP can be decomposed into four main blocks reflecting eligibility, generosity, labor market effects, and demographic changes (See European Commission, 2009).[66]

$$PE = Pensioners * Average\ Pension$$

$$\frac{PE}{GDP} = Pensioners * \frac{Average\ Pension}{\frac{GDP}{Workers}} * \frac{1}{Workers}$$

$$\frac{PE}{GDP} = Pensioners * \frac{Average\ Pension}{Average\ wage} * \frac{1}{Workers}$$

$$\frac{PE}{GDP} = Pensioners * \frac{Average\ Pension}{Average\ wage} * \frac{1}{Workers} * \frac{Population\ 65+}{Population\ 65+} * \frac{Population\ 15-64}{Population\ 15-64}$$

$$\frac{PE}{GDP} = \frac{Pensioners}{Population\ 65+} * \frac{Average\ Pension}{Average\ wage} * \frac{Population\ 15-64}{Workers} * \frac{Population\ 65+}{Population\ 15-64}$$

$$\frac{PE}{GDP} = \frac{Pensioners}{Population\ 65+} * \frac{Average\ Pension}{Average\ wage} * \frac{Population\ 15-64}{Workers} * \frac{Population\ 65+}{Population\ 15-64}$$

---

[66]GDP/workers is used as a proxy for average wages, which assumes a constant share of the wage bill to GDP and a constant number of hours worked over time.

To contain the growth in pension expenditures, reforms need to affect one of these components:

$$\frac{PE}{GDP}=\underbrace{\frac{Pensioners}{Population\ 65+}}_{\text{Eligibility}}*\underbrace{\frac{Average\,Pension}{Average\,wage}}_{\text{Generosity}}*\underbrace{\frac{Population\,15-64}{Workers}}_{\text{Labor market effects}}*\underbrace{\frac{Population\,65+}{Population\,15-64}}_{\text{Old-age dependency ratio}}$$

Eligibility depends on the requirements to receive a pension. For example, increasing the age at which the pension is first received reduces the number of pensioners as ratio of the population over age 65. *Generosity* depends mainly on the benefit formula. Reducing benefits by 10 percent across the board reduces the generosity ratio by 10 percent. *Labor market effects* depend on the dynamism of the labor market. Pension expenditures are inversely related to labor force participation rate of the population 15–64. *Old-age dependency ratio* depends on demographics.

To contain the growth in pension expenditures, reforms need to affect one of these components, which is generally achieved by cutting benefits (reducing "*generosity*") or by increasing the pensionable age (reducing *eligibility* and strengthening *labor market effects* by potentially increasing labor force participation of older workers). If expenditures cannot be contained, the remaining option is to increase revenues via contribution rate hikes.

APPENDIX

6 Health Spending Projections

Methodology to Project Health Spending[67]

Our approach to projecting health spending is two-fold: (1) we assess, but do not reestimate, official projections of countries that have produced them; and (2) we develop a simplified model to project health expenditure for those countries where official projections do not exist. In the second case, the model focuses on demographics and all other factors combined, and illustrates a range of possible spending trajectories under different assumptions about spending growth relative to income growth. This is described in greater detail below.

Projections of public spending in countries with official projections

- European countries: European Commission, *The 2009 Ageing Report* (2009): The baseline scenario from this report implicitly assumes that technological change reduces spending per capita at older ages, which is an optimistic assumption in light of past trends in spending. We therefore choose instead to use the most pessimistic scenario from the

[67]We are grateful to Todd Caldis for sharing the work files from the 2009 Medicare Trustees Report, to Christine Maisonneuve for sharing the OECD expenditure profiles, and to Per Eckefeldt for sharing the data from the European Commission's Ageing Report.

report, where technology and other factors grow 0.8 percent faster than income per capita per year, on average.

- Australia: Productivity Commission, *Economic Implications of an Ageing Australia* (2005): We use the alternative scenario of the report that assumes that non-demographic growth of health spending will exceed GDP per capita growth by 0.9 percentage points annually. The baseline scenario in the Productivity Commission report assumes this difference to be 0.6 percentage points.
- United States: Center for Medicare and Medicaid Services, Office of the Actuary, 2009 Medicare Trustees Report Work Files, and Congressional Budget Office *The Long-Term Outlook for Health Care Spending* (2007); the fiscal impact of the March 2010 health care reform is not included, as the Congressional Budget Office has not yet updated its long term projections to incorporate the reform.
- New Zealand: New Zealand Treasury Department, *New Zealand's Long-Term Fiscal Position* (2006).

Projections of public spending in countries without official projections[68]

- The central element for the projections is a profile of public health spending per capita for 5-year age cohorts.
- We assume that the shape of the average OECD profile is the same for OECD countries and non-OECD countries. For each country, the profile of absolute spending in local currency units for each age cohort is calculated using data on public health spending, the number of people in each age cohort, and the relative spending weight of each cohort.
- The shape of this expenditure profile remains constant over the projection period.

[68]Projections for Canada are based on staff methodology. Staff estimate of increases through 2050 is in between the baseline and the Component-Based Approach in the Fiscal Sustainability Report, OPB (2010).

- Changes in the number of people within each 5-year age cohort based on U.S. Census Bureau projections by country yield spending changes due to demographics.
- An increase in the spending level at a given age (i.e., the expenditure profile shifting up) represents changes in spending due to technology, income, insurance, and any other factors excluding demographics, which, following convention, we refer to as "excess cost growth."
- The baseline scenario is that health spending grows 1 percent faster than projected GDP per capita (exclusive of demographic changes) for each age cohort.
- Given the large degree of uncertainty in non-demographic factors (Cutler and McClellan, 2001) we simulate two alternative scenarios to demonstrate the following possible spending trajectories: (i) an optimistic scenario where health spending grows at the same rate as GDP growth per capita; and (ii) a pessimistic scenario where health spending grows 2 percent faster than GDP growth per capita.
- *Canada*: Data on the expenditure profile by sex and between 1997 and 2002 exist for Canada. We follow a similar procedure as described above, except that we consider spending on men and women separately, using this additional information before aggregating the two to arrive at public spending.

Data

To ensure comparability, we use data on public and total health spending measured in local currency units for OECD countries from the OECD Health Database. For most of the "old" OECD countries, this data extends from 1970 to 2007. Data of newer OECD members generally begins in the 1980s or 1990s. For non-OECD countries, data on health spending (also measured in local currency units) is taken from the WHO National Health Accounts which covers the period 1995 to 2007.

Methodology to Estimate Percent of Increase due to Ageing, Non-Demographic Factors, and Interaction Effect

Increase due to ageing

To calculate the change in public health expenditure due to ageing, we set excess cost growth equal to zero so that the growth in public health spending in each age cohort is equal to the growth in GDP per capita. The resulting increase in spending is then due to changes in demographics alone, with the projected population sizes of each cohort taken from the Census Bureau projections.

Increase due to non-demographic factors

To calculate the change in expenditure due to non-demographic factors, we set excess cost growth equal to 1 percent as in the baseline outlined above but maintain the same age distribution in each year of the projection horizon. The rate of population growth is equal across age cohorts and set so that the total population is equal to the population estimate of the Census Bureau projections in 2050 for each country. We attribute this increase in spending due to excess cost growth or non-demographic factors alone.

Increase due to interaction of ageing and non-demographic factors

To calculate the size of the interaction of excess cost growth with an older population, we combine the Census Bureau projections of population with excess cost growth of 1 percent for all countries, including those with official projections. From this increase, we subtract the increases due to ageing and non-demographic factors alone to arrive at the increase due to the interaction effect. We do not subtract the ageing and nondemographic effects from the increase in the official projections because this residual would also include other differences in underlying assumptions.

Finally, we apply the shares of the increase: due to (i) ageing;
(ii) non-demographic factors; and (iii) the interaction; to the increase in the

baseline projections. This serves as our decomposition of the baseline increases in public health spending in Figure 3.8.

Methodology to Estimate Expenditure Reductions from Health Policies

Provider payment reforms

As an illustration, we assume that fee-for-service payment constitutes 20 percent of public spending which, in turn, averages 6½ percent of GDP in advanced countries. This implies that switching from fee-for-service to prospective payment methods would reduce spending by 0.1 to 0.2 percent of GDP.

Health IT

The expenditure savings from health IT clearly depend on institutional factors, such as how the administration of health care information currently operates. For countries with low levels of health IT, expenditure reductions from increased efficiency may be large, although not immediate. A RAND study estimated that if properly implemented and widely adopted, health IT would yield net annual savings of roughly $80 billion (less than 5 percent of total health spending) while also improving health outcomes in the United States (Hillestad and Bigelow, 2005). However, other studies have been more pessimistic on the size of these savings, partly because providers often do not have a strong incentive to implement health IT. This is because large upfront costs would be born entirely by current users while savings and efficiency improvements would be enjoyed by future generations, implying the need for government incentives (CBO, 2008). If average public spending were 6½ percent of GDP and savings were similar to those estimated in the RAND study, then widespread implementation of health IT could reduce spending by 0.2 percent of GDP.

Table A.5. Public Health Expenditure

(In percent of GDP)

	2010	2015	2020	2030	2040	2050	Change, 2010 to 2030		
			Baseline Scenario				Baseline	Optimistic	Pessimistic
Advanced economies:									
Australia	6.5	7.2	8.0	9.6	11.0	11.6	3.1	0.7	4.1
Austria	6.9	7.7	8.5	10.1	11.6	12.6	3.2	1.1	5.8
Belgium	8.1	8.8	9.7	11.4	12.9	13.8	3.3	0.8	4.9
Canada	7.6	8.2	9.0	10.6	12.1	13.4	3.0	1.1	5.5
Cyprus	2.9	3.2	3.4	4.0	4.6	5.1	1.2	0.5	2.2
Czech Republic	6.5	7.1	7.7	9.3	10.7	11.8	2.8	1.1	4.7
Denmark	6.3	7.0	7.8	9.2	10.2	10.9	2.9	1.1	6.8
Finland	5.9	6.5	7.2	8.6	9.7	10.3	2.8	0.9	4.6
France	8.7	9.5	10.4	12.2	13.7	14.6	3.5	0.9	5.9
Germany	7.9	8.8	9.7	11.6	13.3	14.4	3.6	1.0	5.7
Greece	5.2	5.7	6.2	7.3	8.5	9.3	2.1	0.6	4.0
Iceland	8.2	8.9	9.6	11.4	13.3	15.2	3.2	1.1	5.9
Ireland	6.2	6.7	7.4	8.8	10.2	11.4	2.6	0.9	4.6
Italy	6.3	6.9	7.5	8.9	10.2	11.0	2.6	0.9	4.9
Japan	6.9	7.6	8.3	9.8	11.2	12.8	2.8	1.1	5.1
Korea	4.0	4.5	5.0	6.3	7.8	9.2	2.2	1.1	3.7
Luxembourg	6.1	6.5	7.1	8.4	9.6	10.3	2.4	0.5	4.1
Malta	5.2	5.9	6.7	8.6	10.4	11.7	3.4	1.1	4.7
Netherlands	5.1	5.7	6.4	7.6	8.6	9.2	2.5	1.2	5.7
New Zealand	6.7	7.4	8.1	9.9	11.6	12.4	3.2	1.0	5.4
Norway	6.0	6.6	7.4	9.0	10.3	11.1	3.0	0.9	5.3
Portugal	7.7	8.5	9.3	10.9	12.4	13.6	3.1	0.8	4.9
Slovakia	5.1	5.5	5.9	7.1	8.4	9.5	2.1	0.9	3.9
Slovenia	6.9	7.6	8.2	9.8	11.3	12.3	2.9	0.9	4.0
Spain	5.9	6.4	7.0	8.3	9.8	10.9	2.4	0.8	4.4
Sweden	7.6	8.3	9.0	10.4	11.5	12.2	2.8	0.7	4.8
United Kingdom	8.0	8.8	9.5	11.3	13.0	14.2	3.3	0.8	4.9
United States	6.7	7.3	8.7	11.4	13.4	14.9	4.7	0.8	5.0
Emerging market economies:									
Argentina	4.8	5.1	5.5	6.3	7.3	8.5	1.5	0.4	2.9
Brazil	5.1	5.5	6.0	7.2	8.5	10.1	2.1	0.8	3.7
Bulgaria	4.8	5.1	5.4	6.1	6.8	7.4	1.3	0.5	2.9
China	2.2	2.4	2.6	3.1	3.8	4.4	1.0	0.4	1.6
Estonia	5.0	5.4	5.7	6.5	7.4	8.1	1.4	0.6	3.0
Hungary	6.0	6.5	7.0	8.3	9.5	10.4	2.3	0.8	4.1
India	0.9	1.0	1.1	1.3	1.5	1.8	0.3	0.1	0.6
Indonesia	1.3	1.4	1.6	1.9	2.2	2.6	0.5	0.2	0.9
Latvia	3.5	3.7	3.9	4.5	5.1	5.5	1.0	0.5	2.5
Lithuania	6.1	6.5	7.1	8.4	9.6	10.3	2.4	0.7	3.3
Malaysia	2.1	2.2	2.4	2.8	3.3	3.8	0.8	0.2	1.4
Mexico	3.2	3.5	3.8	4.5	5.4	6.4	1.3	0.5	2.3
Pakistan	0.3	0.4	0.4	0.5	0.5	0.7	0.1	0.0	0.2
Philippines	1.4	1.5	1.6	1.8	2.2	2.5	0.5	0.1	0.9
Poland	4.2	4.5	4.9	5.8	6.6	7.3	1.6	0.8	3.3
Romania	3.6	3.8	4.1	4.8	5.6	6.3	1.2	0.5	2.9
Russia	3.6	3.9	4.2	5.0	5.8	6.7	1.3	0.5	2.4
Saudi Arabia	2.9	3.1	3.3	3.9	4.6	5.5	0.9	0.2	1.8
South Africa	3.2	3.5	3.7	4.3	5.0	5.7	1.1	0.3	2.1
Turkey	3.6	3.9	4.2	5.0	6.0	7.2	1.4	0.5	2.6
Ukraine	4.1	4.4	4.7	5.5	6.5	7.6	1.5	0.5	2.7
Average:	5.2	5.7	6.4	7.9	9.2	10.2	2.6	0.7	3.8
Average	6.9	5.7	6.4	7.9	9.2	10.2	2.6	0.7	3.8
Advanced	6.9	7.5	8.5	10.5	12.2	13.5	3.7	0.9	5.0
Emerging	2.7	2.9	3.2	3.8	4.5	5.2	1.1	0.4	1.9
G-20	5.3	5.7	6.5	8.0	9.3	10.4	2.7	0.7	3.8
Advanced G-20	7.0	7.6	8.7	10.8	12.5	13.9	3.8	0.9	5.1
Emerging G-20	2.6	2.9	3.1	3.7	4.4	5.2	1.1	0.4	1.9

Source: IMF staff calculations and sources listed in Appendix 6.

Note: Under the baseline scenario, health spending grows 1 percentage point higher than per capita GDP growth in each age cohort. Under the optimistic scenario, public health spending grows at the same rate as per capita GDP growth; in the pessimistic scenario, 2 percent above per capita GDP growth.

Patient cost-sharing

The best estimates of the price elasticity of demand for medical care are between -0.17 and -0.31 for hospital services and -0.17 to -0.22 for outpatient care (Newhouse and the Insurance Experiment Group, 1993). However, to the extent that different forms of medical care are substitutes, the effect on overall spending may be dampened. In a study of increases in patient cost-sharing for drugs, about 35 percent of savings achieved by reduction in drug spending were offset by subsequent increases in other medical spending (Gaynor, Li, and Vogt, 2006).

As a rough measure of the expenditure savings from higher copayments, we consider an increase in the share of the cost of outpatient treatment patients finance by 5 percentage points. We assume there are two effects that impact expenditure: (1) shifting 5 percent of public spending to patients (and reducing provider payments from the public sector by 5 percent); and (2) a reduction in the quantity demanded of outpatient care due to a higher price at the point of service. We also assume that average public spending is 6½ percent of GDP and that outpatient care makes up 30 percent of this spending. Based on a price elasticity of demand of -0.2, an increase of 5 percentage points in the coinsurance rate for outpatient care would reduce spending by 0.1 percent of GDP.

APPENDIX

7 Cost Containment in the European Union, Japan, and the United States in the 1980s and 1990s

European Union

In response to rapid growth of public health spending in the 1970s, many EU countries enacted provider payment reforms to contain spending in the 1980s (Abel-Smith and Mossialos, 1994; and Mossialos and Le Grand, 1999). Those that did not pursue cost containment were driven by the desire to extend coverage from a low base (Greece and Spain), but later confronted the need to contain spending in the 1990s. The slowdown was most pronounced in Denmark, Germany, Ireland, Netherlands, and the United Kingdom. Policies targeted the supply-side by constraining reimbursement for physician fees and salaries, pharmaceuticals, and other technology, as well as limiting the number of providers and hospital capacity.

In the 1990s, demand-side measures, specifically increasing patient copayments and coinsurance, were introduced. These charges applied mostly to pharmaceuticals and dental care, but also to ambulatory and hospital services. Their primary objective was to deter demand. Since charges were relatively low, exemptions widespread, and demand inelastic, their impact was relatively limited.

Competition has also been used as tool to increase efficiency. Between 1991 and 1997, the United Kingdom attempted to create an "internal market" to increase hospital competition within the publicly financed National Health Service (NHS). The two major public payers that were designed to drive competition were District Health Authorities and General Practice (GP) Fundholders. District Health Authorities were ineffective at increasing competition because of weak financial incentives that did not allow them to fully capture savings. However, GP fundholding for primary care was more successful at increasing competition. Under the system of "fundholding", GPs were allocated a set budget that could be used to purchase hospital services on behalf of their patients (in addition to the money they were allocated for delivering primary care services directly to their patients). The reform produced a number of positive effects, including reduced hospital prices; lower waiting times; decreased referral rates; and a reduction in prescription drug spending (which was a once-and-for-all decrease). There was also no evidence that GPs selected healthier patients. However, there is some evidence that 30-day mortality rates after a heart attack admission—an important measure of quality—suffered (Cookson and Dawson, 2005).

Japan

Reforms in 1990s brought copayment rates in Japan to one of the highest among OECD countries, to 30 percent in 2002, and separate proportionate copayments were introduced to the elderly in 2000. Medical unit price increases were strictly controlled in the biennial revisions of the fee schedule. Revisions in fee schedule between 1990 and 2006 contributed to a decrease in national medical expenditure by 0.1 percentage point during the period (Jones, 2009). In addition, a new public insurance for long-term care was established in 2000, mandating compulsory premium contribution from those older than forty. The new public insurance scheme aimed to achieve cost savings by shifting long-term care from hospitals.

United States

Managed care was the key contributing force behind the slowdown in the growth of private health spending in the United States in the 1990s, when it grew at the same rate as GDP. Managed care refers to different forms of health insurance organization and management that attempt to control utilization of services and coordinate care in order to lower costs and improve health outcomes. While managed care existed before the 1990s, it became more widespread during this decade. Managed care organizations, if successful in covering a large share of population, can use their bargaining power to negotiate lower prices than traditional private insurance.

Research on how managed care affected health outcomes is mixed, but there is some consensus that managed care has not led to large deleterious impacts on health status (Cutler, 2004). In one sample of heart disease patients, health maintenance organizations (HMOs) reduced expenditure between 30 and 40 percent relative to traditional insurance (Cutler, McClellan, and Newhouse, 2000). These savings were driven by lower unit prices for services rather than lower quantities, and there was little evidence that health outcomes suffered. On the other hand, there is evidence that managed care reduced the adoption of a range of medical technologies (Mas and Seinfeld, 2008). Today managed care remains a key component of the U.S. health system, but it is far less restrictive than in the past, reflecting in part patient resistance to restrictions on choice under managed care (Enthoven and others, 2001). Partly as a result, private health spending has again grown faster than GDP since 2000.

APPENDIX

8 Characteristics of Effective Tax Administration

A proper legal framework for tax administration that provides an appropriate balance between the rights of taxpayers and the powers of the tax agency.

Efficient organizational and staffing arrangements, featuring strong headquarters; function-based organizational design; minimal management layers and appropriate spans of control; streamlined field operations; organizational alignment to key taxpayer segments (e.g., a large taxpayer office); and sufficient numbers of staff assigned to each level of the organization and each function.

A system of self-assessment directed at creating an environment of taxpayer voluntary compliance (thereby minimizing intrusion of revenue officials in the affairs of voluntary taxpayers, while concentrating enforcement efforts on those representing a higher risk).

Streamlined collection systems and procedures aimed at securing timely revenues without imposing undue compliance costs and inconvenience on the business sector.

Service oriented approaches whereby the tax administration operates as a trusted advisor and educator, ensuring that taxpayers have the information and support they need to meet their obligations voluntarily.

Risk-based audit and other verification programs aimed at detecting taxpayers who present the greatest risks to the tax system, supported by effective dispute resolution.

Extensive use of IT to gather and process taxpayer information, undertake selective checking based on risk analysis, automatically exchange information between government agencies, and provide timely information to support management decision making and tax policy formulation.

Modern human resource management practices that provides incentives for high performance and non-corrupt behavior among tax officers as well as develops staff skills and professionalism.

Effective models for ongoing institutional change, including enhancing strategic planning capabilities, building coalitions with external stakeholders, and developing an internal culture that is receptive to change.

An environment of integrity and good governance with transparency of taxpayer rights and required staff conduct, with mechanisms to assure integrity of systems, procedures, staff practices, and to regularly inform the public of organizational goals, plans, efforts, and outcomes.

APPENDIX

9 Assessing the Scope of Policy and Administrative Improvements to VAT

C-efficiency, defined as:

$$E^c = \frac{VAT\ revenue}{\tau_s \times consumption} \qquad (1)$$

where τ_s is the standard rate, is not a measure of the perfection of a VAT—bad VATs can score well. But it can be a useful diagnostic tool.

One use is in calibrating potential revenue gains from raising it to levels found in comparator countries, and therefore presumptively attainable. Table A.6 illustrates, showing for each G-20 member with a VAT: (1) the potential revenue gain from raising C-efficiency from its current level, shown in the second column to the higher levels shown in columns 3–7, while keeping the standard rate unchanged;[69] and (2) the potential gain from raising the standard rate at unchanged C-efficiency.[70] The latter figures assume no behavioral response, and so likely overstate the revenue gain, there being

[69]This is calculated as $\Delta\upsilon((\Delta E^c/E^c)$, where υ is the ratio of VAT revenue to GDP.

[70]Calculated as $\Delta\upsilon = \upsilon\ ((\Delta\tau)/\tau)$.

Table A.6. Potential Gains in VAT Revenue from Increasing C-efficiency

	Current C-efficiency (2006)	Revenue impact (in percent GDP) of increasing C efficiency to…					Revenue impact (in percent GDP) of 1 point increase in the standard rate
		0.5	0.55	0.6	0.65	0.7	
Japan	0.69	…	…	…	…	0.05	0.50
South Africa	0.67	…	…	…	…	0.30	0.54
Korea	0.66	…	…	…	…	0.30	0.42
China	0.65	…	…	…	…	0.44	0.27
Australia	0.57	…	…	0.20	0.56	0.93	0.39
Germany	0.52	…	0.47	1.21	1.94	2.67	0.37
Brazil	0.51	…	0.63	1.44	2.24	3.05	…
Canada	0.50	…	0.21	0.43	0.66	0.88	0.58
Indonesia	0.49	0.04	0.39	0.75	1.11	1.46	0.43
Argentina	0.48	0.30	1.05	1.80	2.55	3.30	0.28
France	0.48	0.36	1.16	1.95	2.74	3.53	0.36
Russia	0.47	0.30	0.89	1.48	2.07	2.66	0.31
United Kingdom	0.44	0.88	1.65	2.42	3.18	3.95	0.44
Italy	0.40	1.62	2.41	3.20	3.99	4.79	0.31
Turkey	0.37	1.92	2.64	3.36	4.07	4.79	0.31
Mexico	0.33	2.23	2.86	3.50	4.14	4.78	0.24

Sources: Staff calculations based on 2006 data from OECD (Revenue Statistics Database and National Accounts Database); and WEO.

[1]Federal GST.

evidence that VAT efficiency falls at higher VAT rates (reflecting perhaps the incentive to greater informality).[71]

The gains from increasing C-efficiency, without changing the standard rate, are clearly in many cases very substantial. Indeed, especially where C-efficiency is low, raising this to comparable levels elsewhere is far more revenue productive than even quite large increases in the standard rate. In Italy, for instance, a one point increase in the standard rate would raise around 0.3 percent of GDP; but increasing C-efficiency to the same level as France would raise around 1.5 percent of GDP.

[71]Ebrill and others (2001).

Calculations of this kind do not indicate, however, precisely where such potential improvements in C-efficiency can be found: C-efficiency itself reflects a mix of implementation and design effects. Progress on this can be achieved, however, by noting that C-efficiency can be decomposed as:

$$E^C = (1 - VAT\,gap) \times (1 - policy gap) \tag{2}$$

So, combining both the VAT compliance gap referred to in the text and a corresponding 'policy gap.' The convenience of this is that estimates of any two elements in (2) enable the third to be inferred.

Table 4.2 of the text applies this approach to selected countries by combining C-efficiency measures with estimated VAT compliance gaps,[72] the policy gap then emerging as a residual.

In principle, the policy gap can itself be further broken down[73] into

$$1 - \textit{policy gap} = (1 - \textit{exemptions}) \times (1 - \textit{rate dispersion}) \tag{3}$$

where the first term on the right picks up the impact of exemptions (which could in fact increase C-efficiency, since tax cascading means that exempting intermediate products is actually revenue-increasing, if they are used by taxed enterprises) and the latter reflects departures from a uniform rate. This requires more information than is currently available for many countries. But in the United Kingdom, for example, overall C-efficiency can be decomposed into the combined effect of VAT compliance gap of 12.4 percent, an exemption effect of 8 percent (determined based upon the other two elements), and a statutory rate dispersion effect of 48 percent—

[72]VAT gap estimates are obtained following a top-down approach to estimate the theoretical net VAT liability for the economy as a whole using national account data and comparing it with actual VAT receipts. This approach does not allow disaggregating the gap by economic activity or sector. Published VAT gap estimates for the EU-15 and EU-10 (the newer member states) ranged from 12–14 percent and 11–22 respectively, on average, over the period 2000–06 (Reckon LLP, 2009). More recent evidence suggests that VAT gaps are likely to have widened in many countries during the economic crisis (the United Kingdom, for example, has estimated that its VAT gap increased by 3 percentage points in 2008–09).

[73]Details and further discussion are in Keen (2010).

Table A.7. VAT Exemptions, Reduced and Zero Rates in G-20 Countries

(In percent of GDP)

Country	Food	Health	Drugs	Education	Financial Services	Non-profit organizations	Cultural services	Supply of land & buildings	Rent	New dwellings	Maintenance of housing	Public transport	Child care services	Water & sewerage services	Children's clothing	Books & newspapers	Domestic Fuel	Agricultural products	Regions	Tourism
Argentina	X	X								X		X				X				
Australia	0.43%	0.22%	0.02%	0.19%	0.11%				X				0.03%	0.04%						
Brazil																				
Canada	0.21%	0.03%		0.03%	X	X	X	X					0.01%					Neg		
China,P.R.: Mainland	Most supplies of services and immovable property, including construction, are outside scope of VAT. Subject to 5% non-deductible Business Tax.																			
France	0.04%	X		X	X	X	X	X		0.04%	0.28%									
Germany	X	X		X	X	X	X	X				X				X				
India	Central government VAT applies to services. State level VAT applies to goods.																			
Indonesia	X	X		X	X		X					X								
Italy	X	X		X	X	X	X					X				X				
Japan		X		X	X	X	X	X												
Korea		X		X	X	X	X	X				X						X		
Mexico	0.69%	0.02%	0.11%	0.15%	X	X	X			2.09%		0.02%				0.04%		X	0.13%	
Russia		X		X	X		X		X			X								
Saudi Arabia																				
South Africa	X			X	X				X			X								
Turkey	X	X	X	X	X	X		X						X		X				X
United Kingdom	0.83%	0.06%	0.09%	0.00%	0.19%	X	X		0.25%	0.39%				0.09%	0.08%	0.10%	0.24%			
United States																				

Country	Total expenditures… ...As % total	...As % GDP
Argentina		
Australia	28.0%	1.0%
Brazil		
Canada	13.4%	0.3%
China,P.R.: Mainland		
France	5.2%	0.4%
Germany	11.4%	0.8%
India		
Indonesia		
Italy		
Japan		
Korea		
Mexico	95.4%	3.2%
Russia		
Saudi Arabia		
South Africa		
Turkey		
United Kingdom	36.5%	2.3%
United States		

Key

- Exemption
- Zero rate
- Reduced rate

Sources: OECD, 2008c, "Consumption Tax Trends" 2008; IBFD Worldwide Taxation Surveys; OECD Economic Surveys; National Tax Authorities; and Ministries of Finance.

suggesting that in this case it is the rate structure that is the most promising route for raising substantial additional revenue. Table A.7, while based on incomplete information, shows that other G-20 countries also make extensive use of VAT exemptions and reduced rates. The associated revenue cost in six countries that publish tax expenditures ranges from 0.3 percent of GDP in Canada to 3.2 percent of GDP in Mexico.

References

Abel-Smith, Brian, and Elias Mossialos, 1994, "Cost Containment and Health Care Reform: A Study of the European Union Health Policy," Vol. 28, pp. 89–132.

Adema, Willem, and Maxime Ladaique, 2009, "How Expensive is the Welfare State? Gross and Net Indicators in the OECD Social Expenditure Database (SOCX)," OECD Social, Employment, and Migration Working Papers No. 92 (Paris: Organization for Economic Cooperation and Development).

Afonso, Antonio, Ludger Schuknecht, and Vito Tanzi, 2006, "Public Sector Efficiency: Evidence for New EU Member States and Emerging Markets," ECB Working Paper No. 581 (Brussels: European Central Bank).

———, 2005, "Public Sector Efficiency: An International Comparison," *Public Choice*, Vol. 123, No. 3–4, pp. 321–47 (Netherlands: Springer).

Ali Abbas, S.M., and others, 2010, *Strategies for Fiscal Consolidation in the Post-Crisis World* (Washington: International Monetary Fund).

Arnold, Jens, 2008, "Do Tax Structures Affect Aggregate Economic Growth? Empirical Evidence from a Panel of OECD Countries," OECD Economics Department Working Paper No. 643 (Paris: Organization for Economic Cooperation and Development).

Auerbach, Alan J., 2006, "The Choice Between Income and Consumption Taxes: A Primer" (mimeo; Berkeley: University of California).

Australia, Productivity Commission, 2005, *Economic Implications of an Ageing Australia*, Productivity Commission Research Report (Canberra).

Baldacci, Emanuele, and others, 2010, "Public Expenditures on Social Programs and Household Consumption in China," IMF Working Paper 10/69 (Washington: International Monetary Fund).

Barrell, Ray, Ian Hurst, and Simon Kirby, 2009, "How to Pay for the Crisis or Macroeconomic Implications of Pension Reform," NIESR Discussion Paper No. 333 (National Institute of Economic and Social Research).

Berg, Andrew, Jonathan Ostry, and Jeromin Zettelmeyer, 2008, "What Makes Growth Sustained?" IMF Working Paper 08/59 (Washington: International Monetary Fund).

Bird, Richard, and Pierre-Pascal Gendron, 2007, *The VAT in Developing and Transitional Countries* (Cambridge: Cambridge University Press).

Blundell, Richard, and Thomas Macurdy, 1999, "Labor Supply: A Review of Alternative Approaches," in *Handbook of Labor Economics*, ed. by O. Ashenfelter and D. Card.

Boadway, Robin, and Michael Keen, 2010, "Theoretical Perspectives on Resource Tax Design," in *The Taxation of Petroleum and Minerals: Principles, Problems and Practice*, ed. by P. Daniel, M. Keen, and C. McPherson (London: Routledge).

Boards of Trustees of the Federal Hospital Insurance and Federal Supplementary Medical Insurance Trust Funds, 2009, *The 2009 Annual Report of The Boards of Trustees of the Federal Hospital Insurance and Federal Supplementary Medical Insurance Trust Funds* (Washington).

Brill, Alexander, and Kevin Hassett, 2007, "Revenue-Maximizing Corporate Income Taxes: The Laffer Curve in OECD Countries," AEI Working Paper No. 137 (Washington: American Enterprise Institute).

Brondolo, John, 2009, "Collecting Taxes During an Economic Crisis: Challenges and Policy Options," Staff Position Note 09/17 (Washington: International Monetary Fund).

Canada, Office of the Chief Actuary, 2006a, *Actuarial Report on the Old-Age Security Program as at 31 December 2006,* Office of the Superintendent of Financial Institutions (Canada).

———, 2006b, *Actuarial Report on the Canada Pension Plan as at 31 December 2006,* Office of the Superintendent of Financial Institutions (Canada).

———, 2010, Office of the Parliamentary Budgetary Officer of Canada, *Fiscal Sustainability Report, 2010,* available at www.parl.gc.ca/pbo-dpb (Ottawa).

Carcillo, Stephane, and David Grubb, 2006, "From Inactivity to Work: The Role of Active Labour Market Policies," OECD Social, Employment, and Migration Working Papers No. 36 (Paris: Organization for Economic Cooperation and Development).

Carcillo, Stephane, Victoria Gunnarsson, and Marijn Verhoeven, 2007, "Education and Health in G-7 Countries: Achieving Better Outcomes with Less Spending," IMF Working Paper 07/263 (Washington: International Monetary Fund).

Clausing, Kimberley, 2007, "Corporate Tax Revenues in OECD Countries," *International Tax and Public Finance*, Vol. 14, pp. 114–33.

Cnossen, Sijbren, 2003, "Is the VAT's Sixth Directive Becoming an Anachronism?" *European Taxation*, pp. 434–42.

Coady, David, and others, 2010, "Petroleum Product Subsidies: Costly, Inequitable, and Rising," IMF Staff Position Note 10/05 (Washington: International Monetary Fund).

Cohen, Daniel, Gilles Saint-Paul, and Thomas Piketty, 2008, *The New Economics of Rising Inequalities* (Oxford: Oxford University Press).

Congressional Budget Office, 2009a, *The Budget and Economic Outlook: An Update, August* (Washington: U.S. Government Printing Office).

———, 2009b, *Cost Estimate for H.R. 2998: American Clean Energy and Security Act as Amended and Reported by the House Committee on Rules on June 26* (Washington: U.S. Government Printing Office).

———, 2009c, *CBO's Long-Term Projections for Social Security: 2009 Update (August 2009)* (Washington: U.S. Government Printing Office).

———, 2008, *Evidence on the Costs and Benefits of Health Information Technology*, Publication No. 2976 (Washington: U.S. Government Printing Office).

———, 2007, *The Long-Term Outlook for Health Care Spending*, Publication No. 3085 (Washington: U.S. Government Printing Office).

Cookson, Richard, and Diane Dawson, 2005, "Hospital Competition and Patient Choice in Publicly Funded Health Care," in *The Elgar Companion to Health Economics,* ed. by A. Jones, pp. 221–32 (Cheltenham, United Kingdom: Edward Elgar Publishing).

Cowell, Frank, 2008, "Problems and Promise of Smart Cards in Taxation," *National Tax Journal*, Vol. 61, pp. 865–82.

Crivelli, Ernesto, Adam Leive, and Thomas Stratmann, "Subnational Health Spending and Soft Budget Constraints in OECD Countries," IMF Working Paper 10/147 (Washington: International Monetary Fund).

Cutler, David, 2004, *Your Money or Your Life* (New York: Oxford University Press).

Cutler, David, and Mark McClellan, 2001, "Is Technological Change in Medicine Worth It?" *Health Affairs*, Vol. 20, pp. 11–29.

———, and Joseph Newhouse, 2000, "How Does Managed Care Do It?" *RAND Journal of Economics,* Vol. 31, No. 3, pp. 526–48.

Daniel, Philip, and others, 2010, "Evaluating Fiscal Regimes for Resource Projects: An Example from Oil Development," in *The Taxation of Petroleum and Minerals: Principles, Problems, and Practice*, ed. by P. Daniel, M. Keen, and C. McPherson (London: Routledge).

Darby, Julia, Vito Anton Muscatelli, and Graeme Roy, 2005, "Fiscal Consolidation and Decentralization: A Tale of Two Tiers," *Fiscal Studies,* Vol. 26, No. 2.

de Mooij, Ruud, and Gaetan Nicodeme, 2008, "Corporate Tax Policy and Incorporation in the EU," *International Tax and Public Finance*, Vol. 15, pp. 478–98.

———, and Sjef Ederveen, 2003, "Taxation and Foreign Direct Investment: A Synthesis of Empirical Research," *International Tax and Public Finance*, Vol. 10, pp. 673–93.

Devereux, Michael, Benjamin Lockwood, and Michela Redoano, 2008, "Do Countries Compete Over Corporate Tax Rates?" *Journal of Public Economics,* Vol. 92, pp. 110–35.

Devereux, Michael, Rachel Griffiths, and Alexander Klemm, 2005, "Why has the U.K. Corporation Tax Raised So Much Revenue?" *Fiscal Studies*, Vol. 25, pp. 367–88 (London: Institute for Fiscal Studies).

———, 2002, "Corporate Income Tax Reforms and Tax Competition," *Economic Policy*, pp. 451–95.

Disney, Richard, 2005, "Household Saving Rates and the Design of Social Security Programmes: Evidence From a Country Panel," CESifo Working Paper No. 1541.

Ebrill, Liam, and others, 2001, *The Modern VAT* (Washington: International Monetary Fund).

Eggleston, Karen, and Winnie Yip, 2004, "Addressing Government and Market Failures Through Provider Payment: Hainan Province in the People's Republic of China," *Social Science and Medicine*, Vol. 58, No. 2, pp. 267–77.

Enthoven, Alain, Helen Schauffler, and Sara McMenamin, 2001, "Consumer Choice and the Managed Care Backlash," *American Journal of Law and Medicine,* Vol. 27, pp. 1–15.

European Commission, 2009, *The 2009 Ageing Report: Economic and Budgetary Projections for the EU-27 Members States* (Brussels).

Feldstein, Martin, 1973, "The Welfare Loss of Excess Health Insurance," *Journal of Political Economy*, Vol. 81, pp. 251–80.

Gaynor, Martin, Jian Li, and William Vogt, 2006, "Is Drug Coverage a Free Lunch? Cross-Price Elasticities and the Design of Prescription Drug Benefits," NBER Working Paper No. 12758 (Cambridge: National Bureau of Economic Research).

Gerdtham, Ulf-G., and Bengt Jonsson, 2000, "International Comparisons of Health Expenditure: Theory, Data, and Econometrics Analysis," in *Handbook of Health Economics,* ed. by Culyer and Newhouse (Amsterdam: Elsevier).

Goldsworthy, Brenton, and Daria Zakharova, 2010, "Evaluation of the Oil Fiscal Regime in Russia and Proposals for Reform," IMF Working Paper 10/33 (Washington: International Monetary Fund).

Gorodnichenko, Yuriv, Jorge Martinez-Vazquez, and Klara Sabirianova Peter, 2009, "Myth and Reality of Flat Tax Reform: Micro Estimates of Tax Evasion Response and Welfare Effects in Russia," in *Journal of Political Economy* (forthcoming).

Graetz, Michael J., 2005, *A Fair and Balanced Tax System for the 21st Century* (Washington: American Enterprise Institute).

Gruber, Jonathan, and David Wise, 2002, "Social Security Programs and Retirement Around the World: Micro Estimation," NBER Working Paper No. 9407 (Cambridge: National Bureau of Economic Research).

Gupta, Sanjeev, and others, 2005, "What Sustains Fiscal Consolidations in Emerging Market Countries?" *International Journal of Finance and Economics*, Vol. 10, pp. 307–21.

Harrison, Graham, and others, "Improving Tax Compliance in G-20 Countries—Contributing to Fiscal Consolidation," IMF Working Paper (forthcoming; Washington: International Monetary Fund).

Hart, Dale, "Voluntary Disclosure Initiatives: A New Tax Compliance Trend," IMF Working Paper (forthcoming; Washington: International Monetary Fund).

Hassett, Kevin, and Glenn R. Hubbard, 2002, "Tax Policy and Business Investment," in *Handbook of Public Economics,* ed. by M. Feldstein and A. Auerbach, Vol. 3, pp. 1293–343 (North Holland: Amsterdam).

Hauptmeier, Sebastian, Martin Heipertz, and Ludger Schuknecht, 2006, "Expenditure Reform in Industrialized Countries: A Case Study Approach," ECB Working Paper, No. 634 (Brussels: European Central Bank).

Hillestad, Richard, and others, 2005, "Can Electronic Medical Record Systems Transform Healthcare? An Assessment of Potential Health Benefits, Savings, and Costs," *Health Affairs*, Vol. 24, No. 5.

International Labour Organization, 2010, World Social Security Report 2010: Providing Coverage in the Time of Crisis and Beyond, International Labour Office, Social Security Department (Geneva).

International Monetary Fund, 2010a, "Exiting from Crisis Intervention Policies," IMF Policy Paper (Washington).

———, 2010b, *Fiscal Monitor* (Washington, May).

———, 2010c, "A Fair and Substantial Contribution by the Financial Sector: Final Report for the G-20" (Washington: International Monetary Fund).

———, 2009, "Macro Policy Lessons for Sound Design of Fiscal Decentralization" (Washington: International Monetary Fund).

———, 2008a, "The Fiscal Implications of Climate Change" (Washington: International Monetary Fund).

———, 2008b, IMF Country Report 08/75: 2007 Article IV Consultation, France (Washington: International Monetary Fund).

International VAT Association, 2007, *Combating VAT Fraud in the EU—The Way Forward.*

Ivanova, Anna, Michael Keen, and Alexander Klemm, 2005, "The Russian 'Flat Tax' Reform," *Economic Policy*, Vol. 20, pp. 397–444.

Japan, Ministry of Health, Labour, and Welfare, 2009, *The Current Financial Conditions and Prospect of the NP and EPI Schemes (Summary): the 2009 Actuarial Valuation.*

Jena, Anupam, and Tomas Philipson, 2007, "Cost-Effectiveness as a Price Control," *Health Affairs*, Vol. 26, No. 3, pp. 696–703.

Jones, Benjamin, and Michael Keen, 2009, "Climate Policy and the Recovery," IMF Staff Position Note 09/28 (Washington: International Monetary Fund).

Jones, Randall, 2009, "Health Care Reform in Japan: Controlling Cost, Improving Quality, and Ensuring Equity," Economics Department Working Papers No. 739 (Paris: Organization for Economic Cooperation and Development Publishing).

Karam, Philippe, and others, "Macroeconomic Implications of Alternative PAYG Pension Reforms," IMF Working Paper (forthcoming; Washington: International Monetary Fund).

Keen, Michael, 2010, "Deconstructing C-efficiency—A Note" (mimeo; Washington: International Monetary Fund).

———, 2009, "What Do (and Don't) We Know about the Value Added Tax? A Review of Richard M. Bird and Pierre-Pascal Gendron's The VAT in Developing and Transitional Countries," *Journal of Economic Literature*, Vol. 47, No. 1, pp. 159–70.

———, and Benjamin Lockwood, 2009b, "The Value Added Tax: Its Causes and Consequences," *Journal of Development Economics* (forthcoming).

——— and Jon Strand, 2007, "Indirect Taxes on International Aviation," *Fiscal Studies*, Vol. 28, pp.1–41.

Keen, Michael, and Stephen Smith, 2006, "VAT Fraud and Evasion: What Do We Know and What Can be Done?" *National Tax Journal*, Vol. 59, pp. 861–87.

Kelly, Joanne, 2007, "Slaughtering the Sacred Cows: An Examination of Reallocation and Review in Five Countries," presented at the Annual Conference of the Association of Budgeting and Financial Management, October (Washington).

Kneller, Richard, Michael F. Bleaney, and Norman Gemmell, 1999, "Fiscal Policy and Growth: Evidence for OECD Economies," *Journal of Public Economics*, Vol. 74, pp. 171–90.

Kornai, Janos, 2009, "The Soft Budget Constraint Syndrome in the Hospital Sector," *International Journal of Health Care Finance and Economics*, Vol. 9, pp. 117–35.

Kumar, Manmohan S., Daniel Leigh, and Alexander Plekhanov, 2007, "Fiscal Adjustments: Determinants and Macroeconomic Consequences," IMF Working Paper 07/196 (Washington: International Monetary Fund).

Land, Bryan, 2010, "Resource Rent Taxes: a Re-appraisal," in *The Taxation of Petroleum and Minerals: Principles, Problems, and Practice*, ed. by Philip Daniel, Michael Keen, and Charles McPherson (London: Routledge).

Lee, Young, and Roger H. Gordon, 2005, "Tax Structure and Economic Growth," *Journal of Public Economics*, Vol. 89, pp. 1027–43.

Liebman, Jeffrey, Erzo Luttner, and David Seif, 2008, "Labor Supply Responses to Marginal Social Security Benefits: Evidence from Discontinuities," NBER Working Paper No. 14540 (Cambridge: National Bureau of Economic Research).

Lockwood, Benjamin, and Guiseppe Migali, 2008, "Did the Single Market Cause Competition in Excise Taxes? Evidence from EU Countries," *Economic Journal* (forthcoming).

Martinez-Vasquez, Jorge, Violeta Vulovic, and Yongzheng Liu, 2009, "Direct versus Indirect Taxation: Trends, Theory, and Economic Significance" (mimeo; Atlanta: Georgia State University).

Mas, Nuria, and Janice Seinfeld, 2008, "Is Managed Care Restraining the Adoption of Technology by Hospitals?" *Journal of Health Economics,* Vol. 27, pp. 1026–45.

Mirrlees, James, and others, 2010, "VAT and Excises," *Dimensions of Tax Design: The Mirrlees Review*, ed. by Malcolm Chote, Malcolm Gammie, Paul Johnson, Gareth Myles, and Jim Poterba (Oxford: Oxford University Press for Institute for Fiscal Studies).

Mossialos, Elias, and Julian Le Grand, 1999, *Health Care and Cost Containment in the European Union* (England: Ashgate).

Mullins, Peter, 2006, "Moving to Territoriality? Implications for the United States and the Rest of the World," *Tax Notes International.*

Murphy, Kevin, and Robert Topel, 2006, "The Value of Health and Longevity," *Journal of Political Economy,* Vol. 114, pp. 871–904.

Myles, Gareth D., 2009a, "Economic Growth and the Role of Taxation—Theory," OECD Economics Department Working Paper 713 (Paris: Organization for Economic Cooperation and Development).

———, 2009b, "Economic Growth and the Role of Taxation—Disaggregate Data," OECD Economics Department Working Paper 715 (Paris: Organization for Economic Cooperation and Development).

Newhouse, Joseph, and the Insurance Experiment Group, 1993, *Free for All? Lessons from the RAND Heath Insurance Experiment* (Cambridge: Harvard University Press).

New Zealand, Treasury, 2009, *Challenges and Choices: New Zealand's Long-Term Fiscal Statement*, Published October 29, 2009.

Nickel, Christiane, Philipp Rother, and Angeliki Theophilopoulou, 2008, "Population Ageing and Public Pension Reforms in a Small Open Economy," ECB Working Paper 863 (Brussels: European Central Bank).

Organization for Economic Cooperation and Development, 2009a, *Taxing Wages 2007–2008,* 2008 edition (Paris: Organization for Economic Cooperation and Development).

———, 2009b, *OECD Employment Outlook* (Paris: Organization for Economic Cooperation and Development).

———, 2009c, *Engaging with High Net Worth Individuals on Tax Compliance* (Paris: Organization for Economic Cooperation and Development).

———, 2009d, *OECD Health Data, 2009*, available at http://www.oecd.org/els/health/data.

———, 2009e, *Pensions at a Glance 2009—Retirement-Income Systems in OECD Countries* (Paris: Organization for Economic Cooperation and Development).

———, 2008a, *Growing Unequal Income Distribution and Poverty in OECD Countries* (Paris: Organization for Economic Cooperation and Development).

———, 2008b, *Achieving Better Value for Money in Health Care*, OECD Health Policy Studies (Paris: Organization for Economic Cooperation and Development).

———, 2008c, *Consumption Tax Trends 2008* (Paris: Organization for Economic Cooperation and Development).

Parry, Ian W.H., and Kenneth A. Small, 2005, "Does Britain or the United States have the Right Gasoline Tax?" *American Economic Review*, Vol. 95, pp. 1276–89.

Parry, Ian, and Jon Strand, 2010, "International Fuel Tax: An Application to Chile," Resources for the Future Discussion Paper 10-07 (Washington: Resources for the Future).

Piggott, John, and Renuka Sane, 2009, "Indexing Pensions," Social Protection and Labor Discussion Paper No. 0925 (Washington: World Bank).

President's Advisory Panel on Federal Tax Reform, 2006, *Simple, Fair & Pro-Growth: Proposals to Fix America's Tax System.*

Québec, Régie des Rentes du Québec, 2006, *Actuarial Report of the Quebec Pension Plan as at 31 December 2006* (Québec).

Razin, Assaf, Efraim Sadka, and Phillip Swagel, 2002, "The Aging Population and the Size of the Welfare State," *Journal of Political Economy*, Vol. 110, No.3, pp. 900–18.

Reckon LLP, 2009, *Study to Quantify and Analyse the VAT Gap in the EU-25 Member States* (Brussels: Reckon LLP).

Saez, Emmanuel, Joel Slemrod, and Seth Giertz, 2009, "The Elasticity of Taxable Income with Respect to Marginal Tax Rates: A Critical Review" (mimeo; Ann Arbor: University of Michigan).

Sancak, Cemile, Ricardo Velloso, and Jing Xing, "Tax Revenue Response to the Business Cycle," IMF Working Paper 10/71(Washington: International Monetary Fund).

Schneider, Friedrich, Andreas Buehn, and Claudio Montenegro, 2009, "Shadow Economies All Over the World: New Estimates for 162 Countries from 1999 to 2007" (mimeo; Austria: University of Linz).

Sennoga, Edward, David Sjoquist, and Sally Wallace, 2008, "Incidence and Economic Impacts of Property Taxes in Developing and Transitional Countries," in *Making the Property Tax Work,* ed. by R. Bahl, J. Martinez-Vasquez, and J. Youngman, Lincoln Institute for Land Policy (Cambridge, Massachusetts).

Shelton, Cameron A., 2008, "The Aging Population and the Size of the Welfare State: Is There a Puzzle?" *Journal of Public Economics*, Vol. 92, Issues 10–11, pp. 2282–83.

Smith, Sheila, Joseph Newhouse, and Mark Freeland, 2009, "Income, Insurance, and Technology: Why Does Health Spending Outpace Economic Growth," *Health Affairs,* Vol. 28, pp. 1276–84.

Social Security Administration, 2010, *Social Security Programs Throughout the World,* different editions (The Americas, Europe, Asia and the Pacific, Africa).

Stockholm International Peace Research Institute (SIPRI) Military Expenditure Database available online at: http://www.sipri.org/databases/milex.

Tanzi, Vito, Ke-young Chu, and Sanjeev Gupta, eds., 1999, *Economic Policy and Equity* (Washington: International Monetary Fund).

Thuronyi, Victor, 2010, "Coordination Rules as a Solution to Tax Arbitrage," *Tax Notes International* (forthcoming).

U.S. Bureau of Census, 2010, *International Database.*

Voňková, Hana, Arthur Von Soest, 2009, "How Sensitive are Retirement Decisions to Financial Incentives: A Stated Preference Analysis," NETSPAR Discussion Paper 10/2009–036.

Wilson, John D., 1999, "Theories of Tax Competition," *National Tax Journal*, Vol. 52, pp. 269–304.

World Bank and Organization for Economic Cooperation and Development, 2009, *Pensions At a Glance—Special Edition: Asia/Pacific* (Washington: World Bank).